Principles of Law Enforcement Report Writing

THIRD EDITION

Gino Arcaro

Niagara College

2008
Emond Montgomery Publications Limited
Toronto, Canada

Emond Montgomery Publications Limited
60 Shaftesbury Avenue
Toronto ON M4T 1A3
http://www.emp.ca/college

Printed in Canada.

We acknowledge the financial support of the Government of Canada through the Book Publishing Industry Development Program (BPIDP) for our publishing activities.

The events and characters depicted in this book are fictitious. Any similarity to actual persons, living or dead, is purely coincidental.

Acquisitions and developmental editor: Tammy Scherer
Marketing coordinator: Kulsum Merchant
Production editor: Jim Lyons, WordsWorth Communications
Text designer: Tara Wells, WordsWorth Communications
Proofreader and indexer: Paula Pike, WordsWorth Communications
Cover designer: John Vegter

Library and Archives Canada Cataloguing in Publication

Arcaro, Gino, 1957-
    Principles of law enforcement report writing / Gino Arcaro. — 3rd ed.

Includes index.
ISBN 978-1-55239-231-7

    1. Police reports—Textbooks.   2. Report writing—Textbooks.   I. Title.

HV7936.R53A73 2008   808'.066363   C2007-907442-1

Contents

CHAPTER 4

CHAPTER 5

CHAPTER 6

CHAPTER 7

CHAPTER 8

CHAPTER 9

CHAPTER 10

Preface

The Reality of Police Report Writing

A message to students seeking police jobs:

- ▸ Writing skills dramatically affect whether you will be hired or not. Poor writing skills will exclude you from being hired.
- ▸ Writing is the skill most often ignored by policing students.
- ▸ Communication skills are one of the "essential competencies" used in constable selection.
- ▸ The quality of your writing will significantly influence the type of police career you will have after you are hired. Please read chapter 1 carefully. It explains the enormous impact that your writing skills will have on your reputation.
- ▸ Police report writing is not just a necessary evil. It is one of the most important elements of an investigation. Report writing influences the extent of an investigation's success. *Every* crime victim deserves the best possible reports.

This book explains an *unlimited system* that may be applied to any type of investigation and its reports. The system is a simple but comprehensive strategy that includes a number of concepts that are used in conjunction with investigative theory learned in other books and courses.

New to This Edition

This revision includes significant changes that will greatly benefit students and instructors.

After considerable research that explored how to serve students better, the focus of his new edition is a report writing model and templates. Students have used these easy-to-use guidelines successfully for several years. They demonstrate how to write any type of police report. Templates have been included for all types of police reports, making the book simpler and more practical.

This text uses a proven police report writing system that has dramatically improved the written communication skills of college students. It has been simplified and expanded for this edition. Additional sample reports have been included in order to demonstrate the application of the system. More information has been provided, in simpler terms.

To help teachers, students, and police officers research recent case law decisions that are relevant to front-line policing, the author will provide an ongoing list of cases and brief synopses at www.emp.ca/arcaro. These case law updates will accompany upcoming revisions of *Basic Police Powers: Arrest and Search Procedures* and *Criminal Investigation: Forming Reasonable Grounds*, which are part of the Arcaro series of Police Foundations textbooks.

About the Author

Gino Arcaro (B.Sc., M.Ed.) is currently the coordinator of both the Police Foundations and the Law and Security Administration programs at Niagara College in Welland, Ontario. Gino has had a unique professional career since 1975 that includes:

- 15 years of policing (uniform patrol, SWAT team, detective)
- college teaching
- textbook writing
- football coaching

His extensive list of publications includes six textbooks, case law articles for *Blue Line* magazine, and articles for *The Canadian Journal of Police and Security Services* and John E. Reid & Associates, Inc. He is currently completing a Ph.D. in Police Studies.

CHAPTER 1

Types of Reports

The goal of this book is to teach police report writing. The starting point is seeing the final product—understanding *what* has to be written.

POLICE REPORT CATEGORIES

There are five categories of police literature that officers are required to write:

1. Notebook
2. General Occurrence Report (GOR)
3. Arrest report
4. Witness Statement
5. Crown Brief

These categories represent the learning outcomes of this book (what you will learn to do).

Notebook

Notebooks are bound, pocket-size books that act as an officer's memory and note bank. Every police officer in Canada has a compulsory legal obligation to maintain a notebook (record daily activities).

General Occurrence Report (GOR)

A **General Occurrence Report (GOR)** is a document that reports any occurrence that is either:

▸ unsolved (investigation is ongoing or continuing), or
▸ solved without an arrest.

GORs are composed of:

▸ a fill-in-the-blank cover page (see page 2), and
▸ narratives, written on supplementary reports (see page 3).

Arrest Report

Arrest reports are the same as GORs, except the investigation is:

▸ active, or
▸ complete, with an arrest made.

Blank Notebook

General Incident ☐   **Arrest Report** ☐

Request for Summons ☐   YOUNG OFFENDER ☐

NO. OF SUPPLEMENTARY REPORTS

DIVISION	PATROL AREA/ZONE	INCIDENT CLASS	INCIDENT NO.

TYPE OF INCIDENT   TIME & DATE OF INCIDENT (TIME OR BETWEEN)   YR. MO. DAY   HAZARD ☐

LOCATION OF INCIDENT

HOW INCIDENT COMMITTED   MEANS (WEAPONS, TOOLS USED)

VICTIM / COMPLAINANT

SURNAME   GIVEN(1)   GIVEN(2)   GIVEN(3)

ADDRESS   HOME PHONE

SEX   YR. DOB MO. DAY   MAR.ST.   OCCUPATION   CONDITION Sober ☐ Intox ☐ HBD ☐ Drugs ☐   RACE WHITE ☐ NON-WHITE ☐

PLACE OF EMPLOYMENT/EMPLOYER   BUSINESS PHONE   (EXT./LOCAL)   HAZARD ☐

REPORTED BY

SURNAME   GIVEN(1)   GIVEN(2)

ADDRESS   HOME PHONE

SEX   YR. DOB MO. DAY   RELATIONSHIP TO VICTIM/COMPLAINANT   CONDITION Sober ☐ Intox ☐ HBD ☐ Drugs ☐

PLACE OF EMPLOYMENT/EMPLOYER   BUSINESS PHONE   (EXT./LOCAL)   HAZARD ☐

VEH. USED

TYPE   LICENCE No.   LIC.YR.   LIC. PROV.   VEH.YR.   MAKE   MODEL

STYLE   COLOUR   VIN

OWNER SAME ☐   ADDRESS

OUTSTANDING FEATURES

ACCUSED / SUSPECT

SURNAME   GIVEN(1)   GIVEN(2)   NICK NAMES   ALIAS ☐ NEE ☐

ADDRESS   HAZARD ☐   HOME PHONE

SEX   YR. DOB MO. DAY   AGE   MAR.ST.   MHT(HT)   MASS(WT)   RACE   WHITE ☐ NON-WHITE ☐

HAIR COLOUR   MOUSTACHE ☐ BEARD ☐ WIG ☐   EYES-COLOUR   COMPLEXION   TEETH   DESCRIPTION OF CLOTHING

BUILD: SLENDER ☐ MEDIUM ☐ HEAVY ☐

HAIR TYPE: BALD ☐ PART BALD ☐ SHORT ☐ LONG ☐ STRAIGHT ☐ CURLY/WAVY ☐ WELL DRESSED ☐ UNKEMPT ☐ BUSHY ☐

COMPLEXION: SALLOW ☐ LIGHT/FAIR ☐ RUDDY ☐ FRECKLED ☐ DARK/SWARTHY ☐ POCK-MARKED ☐

TEETH: GOOD ☐ IRREGULAR ☐ FALSE ☐ VISIBLE GOLD ☐ STAINED ☐ PROTRUD. UPPERS ☐ PROTRUD. LOWERS ☐ VISIBLE DECAY ☐ VISIBLE MISSING ☐

CONTACT LENS ☐ GLASSES ☐

VICTIM/ACCUSED RELATIONSHIP   DRIVER'S LICENCE No.   PROV.   N.R.P. No.

PHYSICAL/MENTAL CONDITION, MARKS, SCARS, TATTOOS, OUTSTANDING FEATURES   F.P.S. No.

CNI CAUTION   V ☐ E ☐ A ☐   M ☐ S ☐ C ☐   CONDITION Sober ☐ Intox ☐ HBD ☐ Drugs ☐   OCCUPATION

PLACE OF EMPLOYMENT/EMPLOYER/SCHOOL/ GRADE   BUS. PHONE   (EXT./LOCAL)

REPORTING OFFICER (FULL NAME/RANK/ NO.)   DATE/TIME REPORT TAKEN   YR. MO. DAY   TIME

OTHER OFFICER(S) ATTENDING   I.D. OFFICER RESPONDING

REPORT CHECKED BY (FULL NAME/RANK/NO.)   CASE REASSIGNED TO   BY   DATE

REPORT CHECKED BY (FULL NAME/RANK/NO.)   INCIDENT STATUS(IF INVEST.COMP.CHECK SOLVED OR UNSOLVED) INVEST. CONT. ☐ INVEST. COMP. ☐ SOLVED ☐ UNSOLVED ☐   INIT./DATE

DESCRIPTION OF PROPERTIES OR INJURIES(INC. SERIAL NOS.)   VALUE   DAMAGED ☐ MINOR ☐ NONE ☐ RECOVERED ☐

INJURIES: MAJOR ☐ MINOR ☐ NONE ☐

SPECIFY ON SUPPLEMENTARY: TYPE OF INJURIES SUSTAINED. TYPE OF FORCED USED. SUFFICIENT DETAILS FOR PLEA OF GUILTY. CO-ACCUSED, PREVIOUS ADDRESS OF ACCUSED, ETC.

FOR NARRATIVE COMPLETE SUPPLEMENTARY REPORT

CHARGES

DATE & TIME OF ARREST   ARRESTING OFFICER

LOCATION OF ARREST   HAZARD ☐

CHARGES(IF WARRANT EXECUTED, STATE TYPE)

NOTIFICATIONS: Y.O.A. - NOTICE TO PARENT SERVED YES ☐ NO ☐

OTHERS: ☐ SPOUSE ☐ GUARDIAN ☐ OTHER - NAME:
         ☐ PARENT ☐ NEXT OF KIN

ADDRESS   HOME PHONE

ARRESTED FOR OTHER DEPT. (NAME)   WHO NOTIFIED?   TIME   YR. MO. DAY

RELEASED TO (NAME/RANK/No.)   TIME

FINGERPRINT DATE   FORM OF RELEASE   BAIL HEARING YES ☐ NO ☐

BAIL & RELEASE RECOMMENDATIONS   STATEMENT TAKEN YES ☐ NO ☐

CNI/CPIC QUERIED? RESULTS

RELEASED BY OFFICER   NAME J.P.

DATE & TIME OF RELEASE   COURT   COURT DATE & TIME

HAZARD REMARKS (MUST BE COMPLETED IF HAZARD CHECKED)

STATS. CANADA   CLEARED BY OTHER ☐ UNF. ☐   INCIDENT CLASS   ADULTS M F   JUVENILES M F   INF.

OFFICE ONLY   DATA ENTRY   DATA VERIF.   DATA RECEIVED IN RECORDS   DATE CLEARED

CHARGE   OTHER

Supplementary Report

CHECK APPROPRIATE BOX

ORIGINAL ☐   MISSING PERSON/ELOPE ☐
ARREST ☐   FRAUDULENT DOCUMENT ☐
INCIDENT ☐   HOMICIDE/SUDDEN DEATH ☐
VEHICLE ☐   OTHER ☐

DIVISION	PATROL AREA/ZONE	INCIDENT CLASS		REFERENCE		INCIDENT No.	

REFERENCE: VICTIM/COMPLAINANT ☐   POLICE INFORMATION

TYPE OF INCIDENT

BUS. PHONE   (EXT./LOCAL)   HOME PHONE   (EXT./LOCAL)

ACCUSED ☐
(EXT./LOCAL)

DATE OF ORIGINAL REPORT

ADDRESS   HAZARD ☐

SURNAME(OR NAME & TYPE OF BUSINESS)

PAGE No.

REPORTING OFFICER (FULL NAME/RANK/No.)

DATE/TIME OF THIS REPORT   YR.   MO.   DAY   TIME

OTHER OFFICER(S) ATTENDING

I.D. OFFICER REPORTING

REPORT CHECKED BY (FULL NAME/RANK/No.)   CASE REASSIGNED TO   BY   DATE

REPORT CHECKED BY (FULL NAME/RANK/No.)   INCIDENT STATUS (IF INVEST. COMP. CHECK SOLVED OR UNSOLVED)   INIT./DATE
INVEST. CONT. ☐   INVEST.COMP. ☐   SOLVED ☐   UNSOLVED ☐

HAZARD REMARKS   (MUST BE COMPLETED IF HAZARD CHECKED)

STATS. CAN CLEARED BY	CHG.	OTHER	UNF.	INCIDENT CLASS	ADULTS M F	JUVENILES M F	INF.

OFFICE USE ONLY	DATA ENTRY	DATA VERIF.	DATA RECEIVED IN RECORDS	DATE CLEARED

Witness Statement

A **Witness Statement** is a first-person narrative that explains the observations and actions of the complainant/victim and/or independent witnesses (citizen and police). It may or may not be written on an official document. Usually it is recorded on ordinary paper with a heading that reads either:

- ▸ "(Witness's name) will say," or
- ▸ "Anticipated evidence of (witness's name)."

Crown Brief

A **Crown Brief** is a book that is written by the investigating officer after an accused person is charged. It is given to the Crown Attorney, who will use it as a guide for prosecution. A copy of the Crown Brief must be given to the defence in order to fulfill a compulsory legal obligation called *disclosure*.

A Crown Brief is composed of:

- ▸ a title page,
- ▸ a table of contents page,
- ▸ a witness list,
- ▸ a summary (a narrative that is the same as the arrest report), and
- ▸ Witness Statement(s).

A Crown Brief is its own category of literature, but it contains other categories (arrest report and Witness Statement).

All five categories of police reports have one element in common—*narratives* (written documents that communicate an incident). Notebooks are *informal*, or rough, narratives. The other four categories are *formal* narratives. There are other types of police literature (such as search warrants), but these five are the foundation for front-line policing.

CONTENT PATH

Narratives convey information called *content*. The content follows a path.

The Content Path

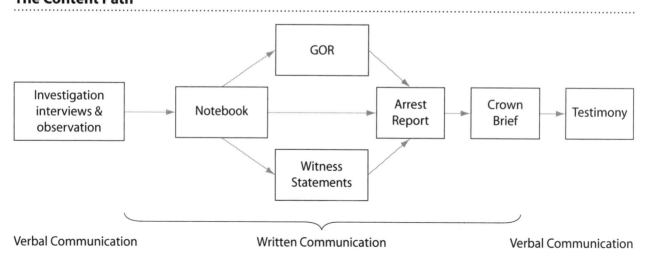

This path is the *maximum* distance that information travels, but not the *mandatory* distance. The starting point is always the investigation, where content is acquired through interviews and observations. The first written document is the notebook. *All* content is informally written in the notebook. From there, the content is transferred into a formal narrative on a GOR and, in some cases, Witness Statements.

If the investigation closes and is solved without the need for an arrest or charge, the path may end. If not, the path continues with Witness Statements, an Arrest Report, a Crown Brief, and potential court testimony if the accused pleads "not guilty."

The path includes two types of communication—verbal and written. The path starts and ends with *verbal* communication. *Written* communication is in between, separating them. One system applies to both types of communication.

THE EBA CYCLE

Law enforcement is a continuous cycle of rapidly analyzing **E**vidence, forming a corresponding **B**elief, and taking corresponding **A**ction.

The EBA Cycle

Evidence → Belief → Action

Report writing communicates the **EBA cycle**.

Evidence refers to information or data acquired or learned by personal observations, interviews with the witness or suspect, and physical items. Evidence leads to a *belief* (e.g., mere suspicion, reasonable grounds). The belief governs the response, or *action* (e.g., arrest, search, or continued investigation).

Policing requires continuous rapid decision making (RDM). The *extent of proof* determines the belief and action taken in response.

REPORT WRITING SAMPLES

Seeing the final product serves as a point of experience for learning and applying report writing systems. You will find samples of the five categories of police reports throughout this book.

CHAPTER 2

The GOS Report Writing Model

GOS MODEL

This book is based on the **GOS model**—a report-writing model composed of **goals**, **objectives**, and **strategies**.

The GOS model serves a dual purpose:

1. It explains the unique characteristics of law enforcement report writing.
2. It guides the writer.

The model shows *what* a report is supposed to be and *how* to achieve it.

Goals and Objectives

Law enforcement is a fast-paced world—one of rapid communication, decision making, and writing. Speed makes law enforcement report writing unique and challenging. In reality, law enforcement writers (LEW) have time to write only one draft. There is no time to revise and prepare second or third drafts. The first draft is the *final* report.

GOS Model

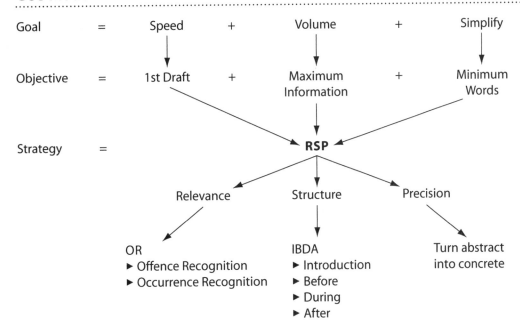

First drafts are usually extremely rough. Most writers need to edit first drafts by reducing words while increasing the amount of information. A LEW has to do what other writers do not—make the first draft the best draft. A LEW must contend with the challenge of limitations on time and information.

Investigations are based on forming beliefs (e.g., mere suspicion, reasonable grounds). Beliefs are conveyed and justified through communication. Many occurrences also involve complicated circumstances. The LEW must, therefore, be concerned with *speed*, *volume*, and *simplicity*. He or she must provide as much completely accurate information as possible, as quickly and simply as possible.

A LEW must:

- get to the point,
- paint the biggest picture possible, and
- be 100 percent accurate.

A LEW must not:

- waste the reader's time, or
- confuse the reader.

A LEW's goals are speed, volume, and simplicity. A LEW's objectives are to provide maximum information with minimum words, through a single draft.

Strategies

The **RSP system** is a communication strategy intended for achieving the LEW's goals and objectives. **Relevance**, **structure**, and **precision** are the major components of this general strategy, which can be applied to *any* investigation and *any* report. It has limitless application capacity.

Relevance starts with **offence/occurrence recognition (OR)**. This law enforcement task requires a specific form of analytical thinking—analyzing a set of circumstances (evidence) and matching it with a specific offence. (If no offence was committed, identify the type of occurrence.) OR is a LEW's starting point, and forms the context for his or her report. OR requires the report to be titled properly (e.g., assault, missing person). If an offence is recognized, the LEW must identify the **facts-in-issue (FII)** that compose the offence. The narrative must be connected to the FII. Relevance guides the LEW to write meaningfully, within the context.

Structure refers to a narrative sequence called **IBDA—Introduction**, **Before the occurrence**, **During the occurrence**, and **After the occurrence**. The *introduction* familiarizes the reader with the participants, the place, the time, and the events of the occurrence upon the LEW's arrival. The information learned is then written in order—before, during, and after the occurrence.

Precision ensures 100 percent accurate interpretation of the occurrence. Abstract language (e.g., "He *assaulted* him") has multiple interpretations. Concrete language has one, simple interpretation (e.g., "Bill *punched* Greg *in the mouth with his right fist*"). A LEW must avoid abstract language and use concrete language.

APPLYING THE GOS MODEL

The goal of this book is to help students to apply the GOS model in realistic cases. Knowing or memorizing it is not enough; it must be applied routinely, just as in front-line law enforcement.

The front line does not always provide the LEW with the luxury and comfort that most writers have. LEWs must write while sitting in cars, standing in public places, and under stressful situations—either shortly after a pressure-packed occurrence, or under the time constraints imposed by the reality of having to move on to the next case.

Communication skills are one of the essential competencies for law enforcement selection and for post-hiring promotion. The goal of this book is to help readers improve their communication skills. But no book alone will dramatically improve a skill—*repetition* does. Practice makes perfect.

CHAPTER 3
The Significance of Report Writing

REPORT WRITING REALITY

How important is report writing in policing? The current police learning system in Ontario, which governs hiring and promotions, emerged from a 1992 study entitled "A Police Learning System for Ontario."[1] The report listed five police jobs—constable, patrol sergeant, middle manager, senior manager, and police educator. *"Communication skills" was listed as the number one learning requirement for each job.*

The study also noted the following:

- "Communication skills" is one of the essential competencies for constable selection.[2]
- A written communication test (WCT) is one of the four tests needed to earn an Ontario Association of Chiefs of Police (OACP) certificate in Ontario *before* you can apply for a constable position.
- These requirements apply for any police job anywhere in Canada.
- Poor communication skills prevent hiring and advancement.

Imagine for a moment that you are a uniform patrol officer on the front line, being dispatched to investigate an endless stream of occurrences. If you are dispatched to only one occurrence every two hours, you will write approximately 1,000 General Occurrence Reports annually and about 30,000 during your career. If you make an average of 10 arrests per month, you will write 120 Crown Briefs annually and 3,600 Crown Briefs during your career. You will have to maintain a notebook to record your daily activities and observations. If you write an average of only 5 pages per day, you will write 750 notebook pages annually and 22,500 pages during your career. This translates into almost 60,000 pieces of literature written during your police career, without even considering a multitude of other documents, such as applications for search warrants. You may actually write more than some professional writers.

Writing these reports will be time-consuming. A 10-minute occurrence or arrest is often followed by about one hour of writing. Then, you will have to verbally communicate your written literature before a large audience inside a courtroom. If you advance to a specialist branch, such as the detective branch, you will read thousands of reports and make critical decisions based on the writing skills of others.

This means that you could spend a large percentage or the majority of your career sitting at desks, writing.

Many police services are large organizations. The criminal justice system is larger. When you embark on your career, you start as an "unknown." As in any organization, you will be constantly evaluated and judged. Opinions will be formed about your competence. The most prominent method of judging a police officer is by evaluating his or her reports.

If you are a uniform patrol officer, you will be dispatched to a complaint. The occurrence may be a minor or a major crime. The circumstances will always be different. If the offence is belated (the occurrence has happened in the past and the offender is obviously gone), you will submit a GOR. It will be assigned to a detective to continue the investigation. In most cases, you will not be able to verbally communicate any information to that detective. Your report will be the sole means of communication to the detective assigned the task of solving the reported crime.

This detective will evaluate your policing ability based on your report, and will pass judgment about you to some extent. It may be as simple as an opinion of "good report" or "bad report," or it may be higher praise or harsher criticism. The opinion will be based largely on how much the detective has to re-interview the complainant to elicit more information. If the detective needs to re-interview the complainant extensively because of insufficient information, he or she will likely voice displeasure about you to someone else. This process will be repeated after every report submitted by you.

Imagine that you arrest an offender after you witness a crime. You will write notes explaining your observations, a Witness Statement explaining the same observations, and a Crown Brief that must establish a ***prima facie* case** (in which all the FII are proved). The Crown Brief will be forwarded to the Crown Attorney who will prosecute the accused person, and it will be disclosed to the lawyer who will defend the accused person. Both of them will evaluate your competence based on your writing skills, and they may convey their opinions to others. Word of mouth is a powerful influence—it will affect your career positively or negatively.

Several months or years later, you may have to appear in court and testify about your observations. Regardless of how strong your memory is, you will have to rely on your written notes, to some extent, to refresh your memory. After you are sworn in, you will be on centre stage in a witness box, where you will speak for a few minutes, hours, or days. The defence lawyer will try to discredit you by asking questions. You cannot run and hide—you will have to answer all of them. More judgments will be made; more opinions about you will be formed.

Traits and Abilities Expressed Through Report Writing

Your communication skills, both written and verbal, reveal who you are and will determine the type of police officer you will become. Your characteristics, beliefs, values, and competencies will manifest themselves in your writing and your speech.

The way you write expresses the extent of the following traits and abilities:

▸ *Knowledge of the law*: Uniform patrol officers must investigate a wide range of criminal offences. Extensive knowledge of the FII that compose these offences is vital. Your reports will reveal the extent of this crucial knowledge. They will show your ability to distinguish what is relevant to the investigation from what is irrelevant.

▸ *Clarity of thought*: Writing is both an exercise and a test of how clearly you think. It demonstrates the extent to which you can structure information and convey it in an organized, coherent manner. Your reports will measure your ability to explain events with precision while eliminating ambiguity.

▸ *Intellectual level*: How people perceive our cognitive ability is greatly influenced by our vocabulary. We are constantly judged by the words we choose. Spelling and grammar are evaluated. Mistakes negatively influence opinions about the writer's intellectual level.

▸ *Work ethic*: The severity and complexity of occurrences vary significantly and dictate the length of a written narrative. A brief or insufficient report of a complex crime reveals a questionable work ethic. Conversely, consistent extensive narrative demonstrates a strong, healthy work ethic.

▸ *Self-perception*: The appearance of your handwriting shows what you think of yourself and how you want others to think of you. The majority of occurrence reports are handwritten because of time constraints. The legibility and type of penmanship is a strong indicator of the extent of pride you have in your work.

▸ *Achievement orientation*: Every report that you will submit is a project. The nature of each report reveals whether you have a strong or weak desire to achieve peak performance. Your writing is directly related to the extent of your desire and commitment to achieve goals.

▸ *Ability to think under stress*: There are two unique aspects of police report writing: (1) time constraints, and (2) non-traditional writing environments. Occurrence reports must be submitted before a tour of duty concludes. Notes must be contemporaneous. Patrol officers do not have the luxury of several hours or days to complete reports. They are often written after a stressful incident and under the pressure to complete the report expeditiously. Additionally, patrol officers do not always have the comfort of an office and desk. They write reports in cruisers, in public places, and other unconventional writing environments. Most submitted reports and notes are the first draft; usually, there are no opportunities to edit and rewrite. Consequently, your police reports will reveal how you think under pressure and stress.

▸ *Attitude toward policing and awareness of the profession*: The priorities in policing go deeper than being able to activate roof lights and sirens. The concept of policing involves an altruism where the interests of "self" are replaced by the interests of "others." Among the priorities is a commitment to provide optimal service to crime victims. From a victim's perspective, there is no such thing as a trivial crime, one not worthy of full commitment and attention. Consequently, the extent of an occurrence report reveals the writer's commitment to work diligently on the victim's behalf. It shows the writer's awareness of what policing actually is. A poorly written, very brief report shows a lack of concern for the victim. Conversely, an extensive, precise report clearly demonstrates a proper concern to serve the victim's interests. The act of reporting a crime in writing can never be viewed as a nuisance, a necessary evil, or a bother that needs to be avoided.

Mastering report writing is a process that, like any other skill, evolves and emerges from training, experience, repeated practice, and maintaining an attitude that it is a vital and integral function of policing. The extent to which you master it reveals your personal commitment to excellence and determines your career path. An understanding that report writing is vital to the investigative process is the foundation from which personal growth emerges; it engenders self-actualization as a police officer.

CRIMINAL JUSTICE SYSTEM COMMUNICATION PATHWAYS

The core function of the Canadian criminal justice system (CJS) is to analyze information and form conclusions or opinions. The criminal justice system is judgment-oriented. The police initiate the process based on information conveyed to them. The information is then transmitted within the criminal justice system through structured paths. Police reports are the principal means of communication within the criminal justice system. Reports convey information in the following pathways and networks.

Police Report Pathways

FROM UNIFORM PATROL OFFICER TO INVESTIGATOR (DETECTIVE—CRIMINAL INVESTIGATION BRANCH)

One of the core functions of front-line patrol officers is to provide the initial police response to a complainant's call for service. In most cases, patrol officers act as the recipient of information instead of a witness to an offence. Patrol officers use interview skills to elicit information from witnesses and record their observations on a GOR. When the severity of the offence or time constraints call for specialist support, the GOR is assigned to a detective, an investigator assigned to a criminal investigation branch. Often, the GOR is the principal or exclusive means of communication between patrol officer and detective. The nature of the information conveyed in the GOR forms the basis from which investigative strategy and decisions are formed and made. Flawed GORs cause duplication, compelling detectives to re-interview witnesses. Conversely, excellent reports prevent the waste of time caused by shoddy reports.

FROM PATROL OFFICER TO OTHER PATROL OFFICERS

When a patrol officer submits a GOR at the conclusion of a preliminary investigation, the GOR acts as the basis from which other patrol officers form beliefs. These beliefs engender decisions made when other patrol officers encounter the suspect described in a GOR. The type of belief formed by other officers is predicated on the precise nature of the circumstances explained. Two types of belief may be formed: (1) mere suspicion, or (2) reasonable grounds. The type of belief formed has a significant effect on decisions made when encountering a suspect after an offence has been committed. Therefore, a police report must be considered as a conveyance of **belief** between officers.

FROM POLICE TO CROWN ATTORNEY

When a criminal charge is laid by the police, the arresting officer has the responsibility of writing a Crown Brief, which includes a written explanation of the evidence that proves the allegation. The Crown Brief is essentially a written record of the investigation and the results it produces. The Crown Attorney forms the strategy for prosecution based on the Crown Brief.

FROM CROWN ATTORNEY TO ACCUSED

The combined effect of section 7 of the *Canadian Charter of Rights and Freedoms* (*"Charter"*) and the Supreme Court of Canada decision in *R v. Stinchcombe* (1991) guarantees an accused person the right to full disclosure. The Crown Attorney is obliged to disclose the Crown Brief to the accused and his or her lawyer, informing them of all the existing evidence in order for a meaningful defence to be prepared. In other words, the police cannot conceal any relevant information or reports from the accused.

FROM CROWN ATTORNEY TO THE TRIAL JUDGE

The Crown Brief includes a **summary** written by the arresting officer, which must establish a *prima facie* case. If an accused enters a guilty plea, the Crown Attorney reads the summary to the trial judge in court. Sentencing is based on the circumstances written in the summary.

FROM POLICE TO WITNESSES

The Crown Brief includes a written statement from every relevant witness who will be subpoenaed to testify at a trial. Although the written Witness Statement itself cannot be introduced as evidence, and the witness cannot simply read from it during his or her testimony, the witness may refresh his or her memory by reading it before court.

BY A POLICE OFFICER TO HIMSELF OR HERSELF

In many cases, a police officer will see events or hear verbal statements from offenders (i.e., confessions) that qualify the officer as a witness. The officer is obliged to write his or her own Witness Statement, which is included in the Crown Brief. Additionally, the officer will record the same observations in a personal notebook. Although the statement and notes themselves will not be introduced as evidence, the officer may refresh his or her memory by reading them before the trial and may use the notes to assist testimony if the notes are proved to be contemporaneous.

LEARNING OUTCOMES

This textbook offers a system that includes general principles that may be applied to any type of police report writing. Every police report tells a unique story. The content of each report differs to some extent; none are identical. There are similarities among occurrences but exact circumstances will always distinguish one from another. Consequently, there is no simple template that will neatly allow officers to merely "fill in the blanks" of a narrative and compose assembly-line reports.

Therefore, the primary skill of report writing is composing the narrative, the part (of any type of police literature) that actively explains the specific, relevant circumstances. In other words, the narrative is the story. A narrative is defined as a written account of the occurrence.

The cover page of a report and headings of a statement are not of great importance; neither requires any special skill or expertise. A cover page is a fill-in-the-blank document that anyone can complete. The heading of a statement simply introduces the witnesses' names. Cover pages and headings may differ from one police service to another but they can be learned in a matter of minutes. They provide only general, sparse information and are comparatively insignificant in relation to the narrative. Novices tend to emphasize cover pages and headings instead of narratives as the measure of effective written communication. The quality of the narrative is the true measurement of writing skills.

Despite the uniqueness of each narrative, there are certain principles that can be applied to the narratives of notebooks, occurrence reports, and statements. Principles are general procedural rules and concepts that make it possible to master communication. The system of principles provided in this textbook serves as the framework for all narratives; the writer's innovation then creates a unique narrative within the structure of the system.

The narrative principles taught in this system can be applied to the five types of police literature:

- Notebooks
- General Occurrence Reports (GORs); also known as General Incident Reports
- Arrest Reports
- Witness Statements
- Crown Briefs

These categories, introduced in Chapter 1, will be examined in more detail below.

Notebooks

Provincial police service legislation obliges all police officers to maintain a notebook that explains daily activities. The notebook represents the first written literature in most investigations. Officers write narratives that emerge from information elicited from complainants or witnesses and their own personal observations. A notebook narrative represents the officer's memory; it will be used to write occurrence reports and to help aid recall during court testimony.

General Occurrence Reports (GORs)

These reports may be called General Occurrence Reports or General Incident Reports. As the name of this report suggests, a GOR has a general use. It is the initial report of a criminal offence, provincial offence, and any other incident that requires a police investigation (e.g., sudden death).

A GOR usually explains an incident that has not yet been solved, and in which no final decision has been made, no final conclusion has been reached, and no arrest has occurred. An incident reported on a GOR often requires some additional investigation after the report is submitted.

A GOR consists of a cover page and supplementary pages. The cover page is a fill-in-the-blank document that introduces key information. Very little skill is needed to complete this page. The cover page is accompanied by a narrative, which is written on the supplementary report pages.

Arrest Reports

Arrest Reports are similar to GORs, with only one difference—an arrest, by definition, was made during the investigation. An Arrest Report is written regardless of whether the offender is charged or released unconditionally. This report also consists of a cover page and supplementary report pages that explain the narrative.

Witness Statements

Witness Statements are formal written records of witness observations relevant to an offence or incident. The Witness Statement consists of a narrative that explains what a witness saw, heard, or did during an incident.

Crown Briefs

Crown Briefs are formal written records of existing evidence to support a charge against an accused person. A Crown Brief is written by the police after an accused person is charged. It is then submitted to a Crown Attorney who forms the prosecution strategy from it. The Crown Brief will be disclosed to the accused person and defence attorney to comply with section 7 *Charter* requirements.

A Crown Brief is composed of the following items:

- a title page;
- an information page, which includes the accused's name, charge, location, offence date, and investigating officer's name;
- a witness list;
- a summary, which is a narrative that explains the commission of an offence and establishes a *prima facie* case; and
- Witness Statements, which are the formal, written statements from every witness who will be subpoenaed to testify at the trial.

In summary, communication skills are vital to policing. Report writing, one type of communication, is premised on communication principles that can be mastered by study and practice. The next chapter discusses the concept of communication and its relationship to report writing.

NOTES

1. Ministry of Solicitor-General of Ontario. (1992). *A Police Learning System for Ontario—Final Report and Recommendations.* Strategic Planning Committee on Police Training and Education.
2. Ibid.

CHAPTER 4
Communication Concepts

DEFINITION

Communication refers to the conveyance or exchange of information and beliefs. There are two elements that compose communication:

1. the *content* (the information and/or belief); and
2. the *method* of conveying/exchanging the content.

There are three ways to convey or exchange content—verbal, physical conduct, and written. In other words, there are three types of communication—verbal, non-verbal, and written.

55/38/7 Rule

Research suggests that usual communication is based on the *55/38/7 rule*[1]:

▸ 55 percent of communication emerges from *body language,*
▸ 38 percent of communication comes from *tone of voice,* and
▸ 7 percent of communication results from *words.*

This means that the usual way we communicate with others depends largely on physical/facial expressions and quality of voice; 93 percent of our usual communication is *how* we get the message across. Only 7 percent is the message itself.

Why is written communication difficult? "Live" communication has the benefit of the 93 percent part of the rule. Live communication is aided by physical conduct and quality of voice to accurately convey context. A writer is limited to 7 percent of a live communicator's capacity. Written communication is restrictive. The exchange is limited. There is no way to use the power of tone of voice and non-verbal conduct.

Writes have to compensate in order to convey information and belief with the same effectiveness of the usual 55/38/7 communication rule.

THE POWER OF VOICE

How important is voice in communication? Research shows that tone of voice "can exert a sizable influence" on the effectiveness of communication. A Cornell University professor taught identical content to two classes, each with over 200 students. The only difference was a "more enthusiastic tone of voice" used while teaching one class. The result was startling. Both sections rated the professor. The class that was taught with the more enthusiastic voice rated the professor as being smarter, a better teacher, fairer, and more approachable. Even the textbook, the same one used in each class, was rated higher.[2]

Voice influences credibility. Remember this study when you testify in court, when you interview a crime victim, when you question a suspect, and when you talk to colleagues and supervisors. Remember this study when you write reports. Your writing style has to match the power of an enthusiastic voice.

Sender–Receiver

All communication has:

- a sender and a receiver,
- interpretation, and
- an outcome.

The *sender's* goal is to ensure that the *receiver's* interpretation of the information is 100 percent accurate. *Interpretation* refers to the receiver's conclusion or belief. The *outcome* is the extent of change that occurs, referring to the extent of action taken by the receiver.

When the sender transmits content, he or she intends for the receiver to understand the entire message. The receiver interprets the content through the interaction of two elements:

1. an *analysis* of the content, and
2. an *evaluation* of the sender's credibility.

During live communication, the receiver can convey simple feedback that informs the sender about the extent of interpretation. The sender has second (third, fourth, etc.) chances to get the message across if he or she was unsuccessful the first time.

Writers face greater challenges than live senders. Writers cannot use actual voice, non-verbal conduct, or an interaction with the receiver to obtain feedback. Report writers have *one* chance to get the message across.

HABITS

Proper report writing habits are formed through repeated practice. The challenge is overcoming the habits of usual, informal communication. The 55/38/7 rule teaches us that we rely on more than words to effectively send and receive messages.

Report writing does not come naturally because most of our communication (such as the growing number of emails and text messages that we send) lacks the formality and urgency of law enforcement writing. Our informal communication habits negatively influence our writing habits. Consequently, we have to learn the formalities of report writing in order to develop long-term positive writing habits.

EXPECTATIONS

Police services expect a post-secondary level of writing from their officers. College and university graduates are expected to write beyond the levels of elementary and high school. This means that the police have zero tolerance for spelling and grammar mistakes. Constable selection across Canada involves some type of written communication test in order to measure a candidate's current level of writing skills and to predict future writing competency. The goal of these tests is to *summarize* the events of a short scenario in a *logical sequence* for the purpose of making a *conclusion* about what happened.[3]

This means that the goal is to convey the most information, with the best words, in logical order, as quickly as possible, for the purpose of conveying a belief.

TIME CONSTRAINTS

The final draft for most formal writing (e.g., essays, articles, books) is not the first draft. A first draft is the first attempt, which is usually not fit for public reading. Multiple drafts shape the content into its final version.

Police officers are expected to submit first drafts. In reality, there is no time to edit and rewrite. Speed is crucial to law enforcement report writing. Writing under stress and pressure is a reality.

WORD COUNT

Students are conditioned to count the number of words to fulfill the requirements of an essay (e.g., a 5,000 word essay). A police report does not depend on word count. It depends on the volume of *relevant* information.

SIMPLICITY

Routine investigation can involve complicated circumstances. Complexity is a reality in front-line policing. The reader wants, and needs, simplicity.

The urge to use "big" words to impress readers is part of human nature. So is the tendency to use a lot of words to convey one thought. We are conditioned to ignore simplicity because it doesn't seem glamorous. For example, "I proceeded to engage in a conversation with the person who the complainant and witnesses indicated may be responsible for committing the offence" is a glamorous way of saying, "I interviewed the suspect."

Turn complexity into simplicity. Say what you mean, and mean what you say.

TOPIC

All communication needs a *topic*. A topic forms the context of communication. The context represents the primary aim.

Police reports have a box on the top of the front page entitled "Type of Incident." This is the topic. It requires offence/occurrence recognition (OR). The circumstances must match an offence (e.g., assault). If no offence occurred, the circumstances must match the occurrence (e.g., missing person).

Every offence and occurrence is composed of elements. Offence elements are called facts-in-issue (FII). The written portion of the report (the narrative) has to contain elements that are relevant to the topic.

Irrelevant information is meaningless. Irrelevant information distracts and confuses the reader, and unnecessarily complicates the narrative.

Stay on track. Focus on the relevant and discard the immaterial.

CONTENT

Content has to be organized and arranged properly to be meaningful and simple. Accurate interpretation by the receiver is dependent on logical order and the sequence of information. The receiver has to know one fact before understanding the next. A progressive stream of thoughts is needed to create a vivid mental image in the receiver's mind.

The participants, place, and time must be *introduced* first, followed by the events *before*, *during*, and *after* the incident (IBDA).

ACCURACY

The sender's goal is to ensure 100 percent accurate interpretation. The only type of language that accomplishes this is concrete language.

Abstract language is defined as words or phrases that have multiple interpretations (e.g., "hostile" or "stole"). Abstract language is made up of generalities that represent an outcome or conclusion. "Uncooperative" and "bad attitude" are examples of abstract language that lack precision. They constitute baseless opinions rather than fact.

Concrete language is defined as words or phrases that have only one possible interpretation. For example, "He picked up the CD with his right hand from the second shelf. He put the CD in his right coat pocket." Concrete language is precise. It allows the receiver to make an informed decision or conclusion based on fact.

Concrete language enhances the credibility of the sender. Abstract language raises suspicion, complicates, and confuses.

NOTES

1. Mehrabian, Dr. Albert. (1981). *Silent Messages*. Belmont, CA: Wadsworth Publishing.
2. Cornell University. (1997, September). "Cornell Study Finds Student Ratings Soar on All Measures When Professor Uses More Enthusiasm; Study Raises Concerns About the Validity of Student Evaluations." *Change.* http://news.cornell.edu/releases/sept97/student.eval.ssl.html.
3. Ministry of Community Safety and Correctional Services of Ontario. (2007). "Constable Selection System: Constable Selection Information Package." http://www.mcscs.jus.gov.on.ca/english/police_serv/const _select_sys/written_exercise.html.

CHAPTER 5
The RSP System

DEFINITION

A system is a general strategy. It is composed of a set of *general* procedural rules and tactics that can be applied to any *specific* situation.

The **RSP system** is a general writing strategy that can be applied to write any type of police literature regarding any type of investigation. It is the centre of the GOS model, designed to achieve the goals and objectives of police report writing.

GOS Model

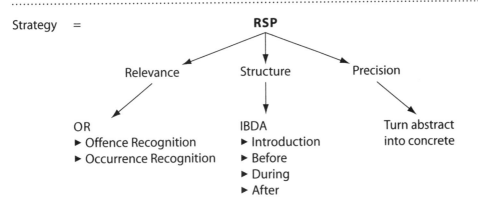

Strategy = **RSP**

Relevance   Structure   Precision

OR
▸ Offence Recognition
▸ Occurrence Recognition

IBDA
▸ Introduction
▸ Before
▸ During
▸ After

Turn abstract into concrete

Report Quality

There is a direct relationship between the quality of content and a quality report.

- ▸ Content has to be acquired through investigation before a report can be written.
- ▸ Obtaining the content is the starting point. This is the data collection stage. There are only two ways to collect data—through personal observations and through interviews (witnesses and suspects). Observations include finding and seizing physical evidence.
- ▸ Written reports are simply a reflection of the content acquired. They *reveal* the information, but do not *create* it. You cannot write what you do not know.

- ▶ Strong content equals a strong report. Weak content equals a weak report.
- ▶ The extent of content obtained depends on interviewing and investigative skills.

Consequently, the RSP system applies to the entire content path (as illustrated in Chapter 1). RSP rules apply to both verbal communication (data collection and testimony) and written communication.

RULES AND TACTICS

The key to applying the RSP system is to understand that its rules and tactics interact and blend together. They do not always occur in a neat step-by-step sequence.

Relevance	Structure	Precision
1. OR (Offence/Occurrence Recognition) ▶ define the problem and solve it ▶ define the topic and identify the person ▶ title the report ▶ identify the elements 2. EBA (Evidence/Belief/Action) ▶ prove the elements (maximum evidence) ▶ form the belief ▶ explain/justify investigative actions	1. write rough notes in a notebook ▶ acts as memory/data bank 2. convert rough notes to formal literature 3. IBDA (Introduction/Before/During/After) ▶ introduce place and players ▶ before: pre-offence conduct ▶ during: *actus reus* ▶ after: post-offence conduct	1. turn abstract language to concrete 2. use simple language 3. say what you mean, and mean what you say 4. source the information 5. assume the reader knows nothing 6. know that you have one chance to write the document 7. be 100% accurate (no clarifying questions required)

Review the GOS model, found on the previous page and in Chapter 2, for a summary of these rules and tactics.

Relevance

Relevance means obtaining and writing about every conceivable, minute detail that has any degree of meaning and connects with any element of the offence/occurrence. Conversely, any information that has nothing to do with the elements of the offence/occurrence is considered to be immaterial and must be eliminated.

OR

Every investigation has a central definable, concrete problem. Every report needs a topic and title. OR requires analytical thinking to match the circumstances of a case with a specific offence or occurrence.

Examples

1. Bill punched Greg in the face, knocking out three teeth—the offence is "assault causing bodily harm."
2. Phyllis has not been seen for 32 hours—no offence can be proved yet. The initial occurrence is "missing person."

OR defines the problem, creates the topic, and gives the report a title. Every offence and occurrence has elements that compose the problem. The writer's goal is to obtain and write a narrative that addresses a solution and locating the person (e.g., suspect or missing person). Finding the cause of the problem and solving the problem are two objectives of report writing.

EBA

All police work involves the EBA pathway. **E**vidence forms a **B**elief, resulting in **A**ction. Observations, items, circumstances, and information are all analyzed, leading to a weak or strong belief (e.g., mere suspicion or reasonable grounds). The belief corresponds to the type of action authorized (e.g., arrest, search, charge). In other words, belief is linked to response.

In order to complete the EBA pathway correctly, an officer must obtain and explain the maximum amount of evidence by addressing each element (FII) of the offence/occurrence. Witness evidence—whether or not a witness can facially recognize the suspect—must be obtained. Physical items used or seized must be identified, and a chain of possession (continuity) described. All evidence collected must convey the appropriate corresponding belief to the receiver in order to justify the action that was either taken or not taken.

"Giving a person a break" is an example of action not taken. Police officers have discretion, but it is not absolute. The recent Supreme Court of Canada decision in *R v. Beaudry* (2007)[1] emphasized the limitation of proportionate discretion. Consequently, when no action is taken, even though the belief of reasonable grounds exists, the explanation for the inaction must be concretely communicated in writing. In other words, the same high standard of justification applies when action is taken (e.g., charges laid) and when no action is taken (e.g., the suspect is "given a break").

In summary, relevance guides police communication by reminding the officer to:

- ▸ define the problem and solve it
- ▸ define the topic and identify the person
- ▸ title the report
- ▸ identify the elements

> **OR**

- ▸ prove the elements with maximum evidence
- ▸ form the belief
- ▸ justify investigative action
- ▸ determine who can and cannot recognize the suspect
- ▸ determine who had physical items
- ▸ describe people and items systematically (general description first; specific description second)

> **EBA**

Structure

Police literature is unique because of time limitations. Speed is part of front-line police reality. **Structure** is vital for the receiver to accurately interpret the content.

Proper structure means chronological order of events. A *before*, *during*, and *after* sequence of events is the goal. Achieving that goal requires a simple path. First, write rough notes in your notebook. Second, convert the rough notes to formal literature in a chronological sequence.

ROUGH NOTES

A notebook is an officer's memory and data bank. It consists of the rough draft of subsequent written or verbal communication.

CONVERT ROUGH NOTES

Rough notes represent the foundation for all reports and testimony that follows. Conversion to formal communication means putting these notes in logical order for the receiver's benefit.

IBDA

Providing order to formal communications involves the following steps.

Introduction

Introduce the place, players, and time. Familiarize the receiver with *who* is involved, and *where* (crime scene) and *when* the event occurred. Include the appearance of the place and players upon arrival, and the initial action taken. Create a vivid image of the location, the people, and what happened upon your arrival.

Before the Event

"Before the event" refers to the *pre-offence/occurrence* conduct and events. Explain all relevant information regarding the players and place. Emphasize the suspect's planning and intention, and the condition and position of victims and witnesses. The period of time is bordered by the first and last relevant moments before the *actus reus*. Pre-offence has a definite start and finish time frame.

During the Event

"During the event" refers to the physical act of the offence or occurrence, representing the *actus reus*. This time period varies in length. It is composed of concrete elements called *facts-in-time*.

After the Event

"After the event" refers to the *post-offence/occurrence* stage. It includes all circumstances that connect the suspect to the *actus reus*, as well as where he or she can be found. It also explains the investigative actions taken. This time period varies—it starts at the moment the *actus reus* concludes and ends upon solution of the problem.

In summary, effective rough notes and repeated practice will result in faster conversion to formal communication. Rough notes represent the first draft; written reports are the final draft.

Precision

There is a direct relationship between **precision**, how accurately information is interpreted by the receiver, and the communicator's credibility. Precise communication is clear and believable. General or vague communication confuses and raises suspicion about credibility.

There are seven rules that ensure precise communication.

1. *Turn abstract language into concrete language.* This rule is the difference between strong and weak communication. **Abstract language** is defined as vague or general words or phrases that have multiple interpretations. Abstract language, because of its vagueness, represents an *outcome* or *conclusion*. **Concrete language** is defined as specific words or phrases that narrow the meaning of the communication to only one possible interpretation.

   ### Examples of Abstract Language

   - offence names or descriptions: assault, threaten, theft, robbed, murdered
   - FII: broke, entered, forced, stole, damaged, weapon, impaired
   - instructions given to an accused person/suspect: right to counsel, reason for arrest, caution, demand
   - accused person/suspect responses and conduct: confessed, admitted, acknowledged, denied, uncooperative, struggled, hostile
   - witness actions or conduct: proceeded, indicated

   These examples represent paraphrasing. Paraphrasing, by itself, has zero evidentiary value. For example, the phrase "Bill assaulted Greg" demonstrates abstract language that states a conclusion. The phrase "Bill hit Greg in the face, using his right hand" demonstrates concrete language—evidence that proves the *actus reus* of the offence (assault) and allows the receiver to form the intended belief.

   Replace abstract language with concrete language; this is the key to accurate, credible communication.

   The following is a list of abstract phrases with concrete language solutions provided to enable precise communication.

Abstract	Concrete
- "he confessed"	use **verbatim** (word-for-word) conversation and direct quotes
- "that's him"	describe the person using a general description followed by an explanation of the unique characteristics that were recognized (e.g., male, 6 ft, green tattoo on left shoulder)

▸ "that's the same item"	describe the item using a general description followed by a specific description; explain the unique characteristic(s) that were recognized; explain the path of possession (continuity)
▸ "he assaulted"	explain the concrete, physical act
▸ "he threatened"	use the verbatim statement

In summary, *do not* paraphrase when:

- conveying a suspect/witness's statements
- identifying suspects
- identifying items
- conveying the *actus reus* of an offence

2. *Use simple language.* Do not use complicated language to impress readers. It is human nature to want to use complex words in order to show off an advanced vocabulary. A police report is not a scholarly, scientific journal. Simple, direct words clarify, whereas complex language confuses.

3. *Say what you mean; mean what you say.* Use direct words to get to the point—"I saw," "he walked." Use one meaningful word to replace a lengthy sentence. For example, "I interviewed the complainant" rather than "I proceeded to ask the complainant a series of questions."

   A police report is not an essay where a specific word count must be met. This does not mean that you should write brief, substandard reports. It means that you should not needlessly lengthen your reports with meaningless language.

4. *Source the information.* Match the observation with the observer. Match the evidence with the witness or location. Connect all information with the source.

   Do not use group observations. When multiple witnesses exist, do not group the observations into one conclusion. Specify *who* reported *which* observation. In particular, every witness who saw the suspect must have an accompanying capacity to identify. Explain whether the witness can or cannot facially recognize the suspect in the future.

5. *Assume a lack of knowledge.* It is important to remember this rule whenever you communicate in police reports. Always believe that the reader has *no* familiarity with the place, participants, and events in your communication. This belief will remind you to be precise and to use concrete language.

6. *Aim for "one chance, no questions."* Remember that you have only one chance to communicate with the reader. Your goal is to have no clarifying questions asked by the reader. The effect of this rule will remind you to be precise and to use concrete language.

7. *Seek 100 percent clarity.* One hundred percent clarity is achieved when the receiver asks no clarifying questions and accurately forms the intended belief.

Predict all potential clarifying questions and eliminate them by replacing abstract, complicated language with concrete, simple language.

Be professional. You are expected to use post-secondary level vocabulary. This means using mature words and phrases (i.e., eliminate slang). However, do not use overly complicated language to try and impress your readers. Use simple, direct, intelligent language.

Do not misinterpret the meaning of "concise." It does not mean "be needlessly brief." It means that you should not use irrelevant information or needless words. Your goal is to convey maximum information with minimum words.

Do not be afraid to write extensively. Do not be influenced by critics who ask, "What are you writing, a novel?" Be specific, and communicate with certainty. Eliminate meaningless words that can confuse (e.g., "He *apparently* took the car"). Communicate with precision and relevance to create 100 percent clarity.

Practise. Write as often as possible. Learn from your mistakes—remember the corrections you are given.

Read. Police organizations have countless experienced writers on staff. Read their literature as often as possible.

NOTES

1. *R v. Beaudry*, [2007] 1 SCR 190, 2007 SCC 5.

CHAPTER 6
Notebook

TOUR OF DUTY

A police notebook is a legally compulsory, pocket-sized bound notebook composed of written, informal notes that serve as the officer's memory, written data bank, and source of accountability. These rough notes are converted to formal written reports and, in some cases, verbal testimony in criminal proceedings.

The content is structured in chronological order. Each daily tour of duty forms a seamless path from the start of a shift to its end. The following is a sample that serves as a minimum point of reference for learning how to write a notebook. It represents a rare tour of duty consisting only of a patrol, with no investigations. This sample illustrates the minimum amount of possible notes.

Minimum Points of Reference for Notebooks

	Saturday, April 21, 2007
	19:00 — 07:00
18:23	Report for duty
	roads: snow covered and wet
	visibility: clear, light snow
18:30	Briefing started
	patrol district: 12-34
	cruiser number 362
	partner: Cst. G. Schmidt (passenger)
18:40	Briefing complete
18:43	Searched cruiser——negative results
18:45	10-8
23:00	10-7 51 Division 10-43
23:45	10-8
03:15	10-7 51 Division 10-43
04:00	10-8
06:45	10-7 51 Division 10-43
	Off duty
	Cst. N. Huddle

This tour of duty flowed continuously from start to finish. No investigations occurred. This officer responded to no calls for service, stopped no cars or pedestrians, laid no charges, and made no arrests. The entire tour of duty consisted of general patrol with two lunch breaks.

The following is a translation of the 12 elements that compose the sample tour of duty.

1. The date was Saturday, April 21, 2007.
2. 19:00 – 07:00 represents the 24-hour clock version of the officer's tour of duty—a 12-hour shift (7:00 p.m. to 7:00 a.m.).
3. At 18:23, the officer reported for duty. This is the starting point of the officer's record of accountability; written notes explain a seamless path of *times*, *places*, and *activities* that account for where the officer was and what the officer did.
4. At 18:30, "briefing" started. **Briefing** is a platoon meeting where uniform constables receive assignments and instructions from a supervisor (usually a patrol sergeant). In this case, the officer was assigned to patrol district 12-34, in cruiser number 362, and to *double crew* with Constable G. Schmidt. The author of these notes drove; Constable G. Schmidt was the passenger. *Both* officers must make separate notes and keep a separate notebook.
5. Briefing ended at 18:40.
6. At 18:43, the officers entered the cruiser. Before starting patrol, they searched it for safety reasons, ensuring that no items had been concealed by previous prisoners that could be found and used by new prisoners.
7. At 18:45, they began general patrol. "10-8" is the **10-code language** that means "**in service**"—the officers are available to respond to calls for service. At this point, no specific notes are made if the officers conduct general patrol only. In other words, officers do not record the path of patrol.

   10-8 is the first patrol event. It means that the officers started general patrol. An officer may write "in service" instead if his or her police service policy dictates. Otherwise, he or she should use the 10-code to save time and writing.

   After 10-8 is noted, there must be an arrival of a second event. In this minimum point of reference, there were no investigations. The second event was a lunch break.

8. At 23:00, the officers arrived at 51 Division (name of police station).

   10-7 refers to "**out of service**," and means "arrived at [place] and is not available to respond to calls for service." "Out of service" may be used, but the 10-code is simpler. 10-43 means "lunch break."

9. At 23:45, the lunch break ended and general patrol resumed. "10-8" is a simple note that replaces this entire sentence.
10. At 03:15, the officer arrived at the police station for the second lunch break.
11. At 04:00, general patrol resumed.
12. At 06:45, general patrol ended. The officer arrived at the police station and booked off duty.
13. Each tour of duty ends with the officer's rank and name.

Although this tour of duty is a rarity, it gives you a point of reference—a starting point for learning how to write a police notebook. This sample illustrated a chronological sequence of events that accounts for the officer's activities and general whereabouts.

RELEVANT LAWS

Maintaining a daily notebook is a legal requirement, mandated both by the provincial statutes that govern policing and by the rules and regulations that form the policies of individual police services. A notebook is the property of (is owned by) the police service that issues it, not the officer who carries it. This rule applies to currently serving and former officers. For this reason, the contents of a notebook are considered to be "records" under provincial statutes that govern freedom of information and may be accessed by the public. For example, section 4(1) of the *Municipal Freedom of Information and Protection of Privacy Act* of Ontario[1] states that "every person has a right of access" to a record or part of a record (such as police notebooks) unless the request is "frivolous and vexatious" or falls within one of 10 listed exemptions under sections 6–15. Two exceptions that refer to law enforcement include:

1. interference with a law enforcement matter, and
2. personal information.

Disclosure of a police notebook may be refused if the information will:

- interfere with an investigation;
- reveal investigative techniques and procedures;
- identify a confidential informant;
- endanger the life or the safety of any person;
- endanger the security of a building or vehicle;
- facilitate the escape of a lawfully detained person;
- jeopardize the security of a correctional facility;
- facilitate the commission of an unlawful act; or
- hamper the control of crime.[2]

Personal information is defined as recorded information about an identifiable individual, including:

- race, national or ethnic origin, colour, religion, age, gender, sexual orientation, or marital status;
- address, phone number, fingerprints, or blood type;
- education;
- medical or psychiatric history;
- criminal history;
- employment history;
- financial transactions;
- personal opinions or views of the individual, except if they relate to another individual; and
- the views or opinions of another individual about the individual.[3]

The information recorded in a police officer's notebook is not the personal property of the officer. An exception to this is recorded information relating to an investigation of the officer's conduct.[4]

STRUCTURE

Notebooks involve *structure* and *content*. Structure includes format and concepts that govern the appearance of how notes should look. There are 21 general rules that apply to notebook structure.

1. Use a bound, pocket-size notebook

The purpose of the binding on a bound notebook is to help prove the credibility of the content during court testimony. It shows that pages were not inserted, removed, or replaced—actions that are prohibited. The binding itself will certainly not prove credibility; it simply helps the process. Theoretically, it does not matter where you write notes; looseleaf pages are acceptable because notes are only a means of refreshing memory and facilitating recall. The notes themselves are not introduced as evidence at a trial; the officer must verbally testify under oath about the contents. In other words, he or she refers to the notes but the verbal testimony is the evidence that matters. The verbal testimony is the specific target of credibility evaluation. Notes are indirectly evaluated for credibility because they are the source of the recall that engenders verbal testimony. A bound notebook helps refute defence cross-examination tactics and insinuations that suggest notes were made just before the court trial or some other type of sinister act that would bring the notes into disrepute. During the history of policing, it has been fashionable for excessive and unwarranted suspicion to be directed toward police notes and testimony. Consequently, this and subsequent rules are intended to elevate the credibility of notes and testimony.

2. Write on every line

No line of a page should be blank. The only blank lines should be a single blank line separating days; the last line at the end of one tour of duty is left blank to separate that day from the next. Blank lines are avoided to prevent suspicion that notes were entered after a tour of duty was completed.

3. Errors must be readable

Mistakes are expected when anything is written. However, errors in police notebooks must be readable to prevent suspicion of altering notes after they are written. Draw one line through the error and initial it. Do not obliterate the error or white it out, and do not rewrite a notebook to change original pages.

4. Retain original notes of personal observations

A notebook is relatively small and often awkward to write on. Officers commonly use 8½" × 11" looseleaf paper on clipboards to record initial notes; the original notes are used to transcribe observations into the notebook. Do the originals have to be kept? The answer depends on what type of note was recorded. There are two types of notes:

1. hearsay, and
2. personal observations.

Generally, a witness may testify only about what he or she perceives with his or her senses—personal observations. Hearsay evidence refers to observations not perceived by one's own senses; hearsay is information reported by the person who saw or heard it. Generally, hearsay evidence is inadmissible. The hearsay rule has been relaxed during the past decade; exceptions have been added as a result of case law decisions. Yet, officers will not be permitted to testify about most information that they receive from eyewitnesses.

Consequently, original notes that represent hearsay evidence generally do not have to be kept. Notes that represent personal observations do have to be kept. For example, if you write down the licence plate of a car that you observed committing an offence or verbatim conversation with a suspect or accused person on paper other than a notebook, keep the original notes. They may be stored in a file with the Crown Brief or attached to the notebook.

5. Record only what you actually remember

This is a common-sense rule that needs little explanation. Perjury is an indictable offence with a maximum penalty of 14 years' imprisonment.

6. When multiple officers make observations in one incident, each officer must make independent notes (separate individual notes)

One officer cannot simply sign another officer's notes or use another officer's notes to testify from. The best example is the questioning of an accused person by more than one officer. The Ontario Court of Appeal, in *R v. Barrett* (1993),[5] ruled that every officer present during an interrogation must make independent notes. Different officers' notes are not expected to be the same. Memories and recall abilities are different. Yet there has been a tendency among novices to believe that officers' observations must be the same to prove personal and group credibility. It is a misguided notion to believe that judges expect and believe that two or more people saw and heard precisely the same minute details of an event or conversation. This, then, raises the issue of officers discussing observations prior to making notes.

Collaborating on notes refers to discussing what was done and said during an event or conversation. Collaboration among officers is inevitable and acceptable if the notes that are written after the collaboration reflect precisely what each individual officer honestly remembers. According to case law, a police officer may discuss observations with another officer, prior to notebook writing, as long as the officer can testify under oath that the personal observations are the truth and not fabricated.[6]

The purpose of discussion is to help recall. If it triggers memory and information is recalled, then the collaborated notes can be recorded. There is nothing sinister about one officer triggering another officer's memory if that detail or fact can honestly be remembered. Collaboration is unlawful if an officer records notes and subsequently testifies under oath intentionally about facts that are not honestly remembered.

7. Record all daily tasks chronologically

A police notebook is a journal composed of a written record explaining the tasks performed during each daily tour of duty. It resembles a diary that includes accounts of one day followed in order by subsequent days (whether working or not).

Each tour of duty resembles a time sheet that chronologically records all relevant police tasks performed. Each daily record should allow the officer to explain exactly what the officer did, when it was done, and where it occurred. It should be able to generally explain one's whereabouts and therefore represents performance accountability.

Although there are a multitude of tasks performed, the following is a list of the most common ones that **must** be included:

- all complaints investigated, regardless of severity, including federal statutes, provincial offences, and municipal bylaw complaints;
- motor vehicle collision investigations;
- arrests;
- suspects interviewed;
- witnesses interviewed;
- vehicle stops and action taken;
- physical evidence seized;
- tickets issued;
- personal observations relevant to any investigation;
- crime scenes guarded;
- escorts;
- searches conducted of persons and places;
- times of arrival at each task location and time of departure; and
- any relevant activity at any place, including a police station, that justified absence from general patrol.

General patrol is the core function of officers in the uniform patrol branch. It is impracticable to record every street or location specifically patrolled. Consequently, general patrol is noted between the departure time of one task and the arrival time of the next one. In other words, the space between specific tasks is simply noted as general patrol without specifying areas travelled.

8. Title each day

Write the day and date regardless of whether you are working or not. If you are not working, write "off duty." If you are working, enter the scheduled hours of work followed by the time you reported for duty and the road conditions and visibility.

9. Use the 24-hundred hour system to record times

All relevant times are recorded in the left margin. The 24-hundred hour system is the preferred method of recording times. The system begins at 00:01 hours (12:01 a.m.) and finishes at 24:00 hours (12:00 midnight). Here are a few examples:

05:00	_____	(5:00 a.m.)
09:30	_____	(9:30 a.m.)
12:00	_____	(12:00 noon)
17:00	_____	(5:00 p.m.)
21:30	_____	(9:30 p.m.)

No law prevents the conventional a.m./p.m. system from being used.

10. Record "briefing" time and relevant briefing information

"Briefing" is a platoon meeting conducted prior to the beginning of a tour of duty. A supervisor informs patrol officers of assignments and relevant information pertaining to investigations being conducted. Record the time briefing commenced followed by the assigned patrol area, cruiser number, and partner's name (if one is assigned). The remainder of the information may be lengthy. It may be entered on that page or on paper external to the notebook, for convenience.

11. Record all "in-service" times

"In service" means that an officer is on general patrol and is available to respond to calls for service. For simplicity, use "10-8," the corresponding 10-code short form. The first 10-8 time starts a pathway that ends at the completion of that tour of duty. Record each subsequent in-service time after an "out-of-service" investigation ends.

12. Record all "out-of-service" times and places

"Out of service" means that an officer has arrived at a specific place to conduct an investigation, and is not available to respond to calls for service. There are two types of "out of service":

1. "10-7," meaning "arrived at [a place]"
2. "10-38," meaning "stopped a while at [a place]"

Both represent arrivals and non-availability for other calls for service. The only difference is the anticipated amount of time spent at the location.

- "10-7" generally requires more investigative time, and refers to a *reactive* investigation.
- "10-38" generally requires less time, and refers to a *proactive* investigation.

An officer must record the place where he or she went out of service and why (reason).

EXAMPLE

10-7   5000 Barton St.
         Re: Belated break, enter, and theft (*reactive investigation*)

10-38   Adelaide St. and King St.
         2005 Mazda, Ont. Reg. APRP 362
         Re: Speeding (*proactive investivation*)

At the conclusion of the investigation, record "10-8." A notebook must have a continuous stream of "in-service" and "out-of-service" notations. The corresponding times will account for where you were, how much time you were there, and what you did.

The following sample illustrates the in-service/out-of-service path. The activity was not recorded.

EXAMPLE

18:45	10-8
18:53	10-7 362 Yonge St.
	Re: Alarm
18:59	10-8
19:04	10-38 Lakeshore Rd. and King St.
	2005 GMC, Ont. Reg. AWHC 362
	Re: Fail to stop for red light
19:16	10-8

13. Conversations with accused persons or potential suspects are recorded verbatim

Confessions, when admissible, are the best evidence to prove guilt. The prosecution has the onus of proving that confessions were voluntarily made. Determining the admissibility of a confession requires a trial judge's analysis of what was said prior to and during the confession. Consequently, all conversations with accused persons must be recorded verbatim, meaning word-for-word direct quotes. These conversations include formal interrogations in a police station or in public, such as at the scene of an arrest or while en route to the police station. All dialogue must be included, even unrelated conversation and exculpatory remarks—that is, denials and alibis. This rule applies to conversations with persons who are potential suspects, referring to persons who have not been charged yet and when reasonable grounds do not exist to believe that the person committed the offence.

14. Record "reported observations" precisely

The most common out-of-service investigative notes emerge from reactive investigations—investigations that you did not find being committed. Instead, you responded to a call for service.

These investigations involve the reported observations of two classifications of witnesses:

1. complainant/victim; and
2. **independent witness** (a non-complainant, non-victim).

When you receive information from a witness, you are the recipient of *hearsay* evidence. Generally, you cannot testify at a trial about what witnesses reported to you.

However, precise notes are needed for these reasons:

- ‣ to convert to formal written reports;
- ‣ in situations where hearsay evidence is admissible (during bail hearings and **ex parte** hearings; the Supreme Court of Canada decision in *R v. Khan* (1990)[7] expanded on the types of situations where hearsay is admissible); and
- ‣ in case the witness intentionally misleads you and is charged with Public Mischief, Obstruct Justice, or Obstruct Police.

Witness reports do not have to be recorded verbatim. Verbatim notes apply to suspects and accused persons only. Witness observations are recorded precisely and written in narrative form.

15. Record your own witness observations precisely

A police officer is a witness when testifying about:

- proactive investigations, where the officer finds an offence being committed;
- **circumstantial evidence**, including describing a crime scene upon arrival; and
- arrest, search, and instructions to an accused (the reason for the arrest, their right to council, caution, breath demands).

Concrete verbatim notes are needed to prove that the arrest and searches were lawful, and that instructions were given and understood. Proper notes help elevate your credibility and positively affect admissibility of evidence.

16. Record precise physical appearance of crime scenes and items seized

Recording the appearance of a crime scene, as it looks upon arrival of the first officer, is crucial for accurate conclusions and to facilitate the admissibility of seized physical items. After the time of arrival is recorded, a written description of the scene's appearance is required, accompanied by a rough diagram. Afterward, all relevant events must be recorded, including the names of authorized persons who entered the crime scene, the route used, what was altered, and the time of departure. Seized items require time of seizure, description of item, and relevant information and times relating to continuity of the seized item.

17. Record off-duty time at conclusion of the tour of duty

Often, the time of arrival at the police station will coincide with the off-duty time; in these instances, record the 10-code for "out of service" followed by "off duty" after the arrival time entry. In other cases, other tasks need completion after arriving at the police station; simply record the "out of service" time followed by an explanation of the task performed and the off-duty time afterward.

18. Summarize the daily performance

Many police tasks can be quantified. A brief summary of the number of complaints, arrests, tickets, and persons checked help recall when the officer is required to be accountable for his or her actions.

19. Sign the notebook

20. Have a supervisor sign on the line following your signature

21. Leave one space blank before recording the next date

Structure Sample

The following is a sample of how to apply the rules of structure with only two out-of-service investigations.

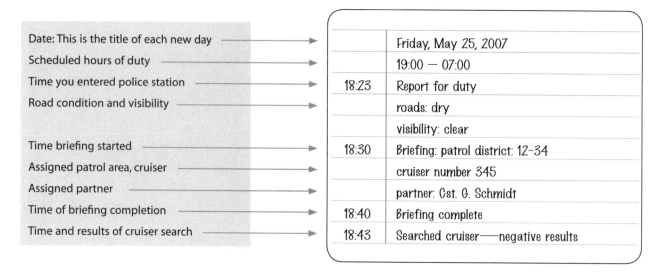

		Friday, May 25, 2007
		19:00 — 07:00
	18:23	Report for duty
		roads: dry
		visibility: clear
	18:30	Briefing: patrol district: 12-34
		cruiser number 345
		partner: Cst. G. Schmidt
	18:40	Briefing complete
	18:43	Searched cruiser—negative results

Date: This is the title of each new day

Scheduled hours of duty

Time you entered police station

Road condition and visibility

Time briefing started

Assigned patrol area, cruiser

Assigned partner

Time of briefing completion

Time and results of cruiser search

"In service": Time general patrol begins; use appropriate 10-code. Continue on general patrol until first task.

Start of Task #1: First out-of-service investigation. Record the arrival time, location, and nature of call, complainant's relevant personal information, and observations.

Explain any circumstances that cause suspicion of an offender.

18:45	10-8
19:10	10-7 3001 Queen St.
	Re: break, enter, and theft
	Complainant: Hec Creighton
	Address: same
	D.O.B.: 30-01-02
	Phone: (404) 240-3001
	Mr. Creighton is the owner of the house. He left for work at 07:45 hrs today and he locked all the doors.
	Returned home at 19:00 hrs.
	Point of entry: back door (south side). Inside wooden door was open. The door and frame were splintered. Wood fragments were on the floor, inside that entrance. Seven dents were on the door near the doorknob, about 2 m from the ground.
	Only item stolen:
	20" Sony TV—silver and black
	- serial number 04-3001-2002
	- volume button missing
	- value: $500.00
	- stolen from living room
	nothing else touched or moved
	no suspects

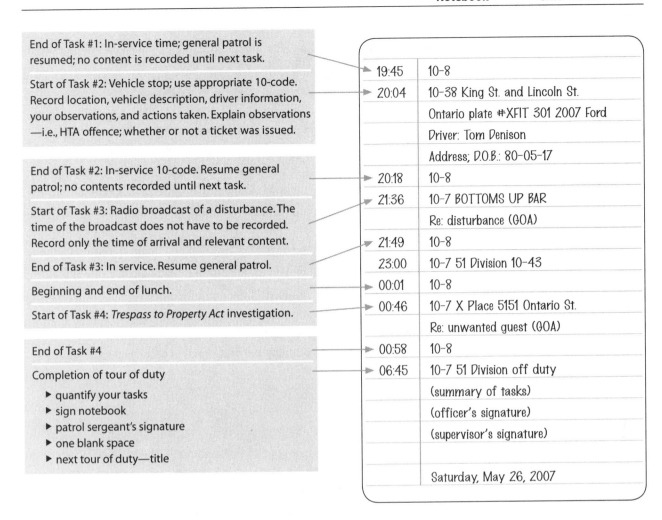

End of Task #1: In-service time; general patrol is resumed; no content is recorded until next task.	19:45	10-8
Start of Task #2: Vehicle stop; use appropriate 10-code. Record location, vehicle description, driver information, your observations, and actions taken. Explain observations —i.e., HTA offence; whether or not a ticket was issued.	20:04	10-38 King St. and Lincoln St.
		Ontario plate #XFIT 301 2007 Ford
		Driver: Tom Denison
		Address; D.O.B.: 80-05-17
End of Task #2: In-service 10-code. Resume general patrol; no contents recorded until next task.	20:18	10-8
Start of Task #3: Radio broadcast of a disturbance. The time of the broadcast does not have to be recorded. Record only the time of arrival and relevant content.	21:36	10-7 BOTTOMS UP BAR
		Re: disturbance (GOA)
End of Task #3: In service. Resume general patrol.	21:49	10-8
	23:00	10-7 51 Division 10-43
Beginning and end of lunch.	00:01	10-8
Start of Task #4: *Trespass to Property Act* investigation.	00:46	10-7 X Place 5151 Ontario St.
		Re: unwanted guest (GOA)
End of Task #4	00:58	10-8
Completion of tour of duty	06:45	10-7 51 Division off duty
▸ quantify your tasks		(summary of tasks)
▸ sign notebook		(officer's signature)
▸ patrol sergeant's signature		(supervisor's signature)
▸ one blank space		
▸ next tour of duty—title		Saturday, May 26, 2007

NARRATIVE

After notes are recorded to complete the cover page of a report, the focus shifts to narrative information. The narrative is the story that explains the circumstances of the occurrence. It is the most important part of a police report. The information needed to write a narrative is first recorded in a notebook. It becomes the source of information used to write the narrative of a report.

Narrative notes are derived from observations. Observations refer to what is seen or heard by an individual—in other words, what is perceived through one's own senses. They include seeing a series of acts, seeing an item that is later seized, and hearing words spoken by a suspect. Observations relevant to an offence are made by both citizens and investigating officers. They may occur before, during, or after the offence. Those made by citizens emerge from the officer's interviewing skills. Officer's observations are reliant on memory recall.

Observations are classified into three groups: eyewitness, corroborative, and recipient of confessions or incriminating verbal statements. **Eyewitness observations** are made when the ***actus reus*** of the offence is seen, meaning the physical act that occurred during the offence. Corroborative observations are supporting observations of relevant events that occur before or after the offence. Incriminating verbal statements made by offenders may be heard before, during, or after an offence.

During a reactive investigation, the investigating officer does not make eyewitness observations. Instead, the officer:

- elicits information from others in relation to the three stages of the offence; and
- makes corroborative observations, those seen after the offence, including appearance of the crime scene, items found, and conversations with suspects.

During a proactive investigation, the officer makes eyewitness observations of the *actus reus*. Citizens may also provide eyewitness and corroborative observations. Common examples of proactive investigations include impaired driving and disturbances.

A fundamental of notebook narrative writing emerges from the seven elements upon which the criminal justice system is premised.

1. Charging an offender represents a formal *allegation*.
2. The Crown has the *onus* to prove all formal allegations.
3. Allegations are proved by *evidence*.
4. Evidence is introduced through witness *observations*.
5. *Precise, relevant* observations constitute evidence.
6. Evidence is analyzed by the *judge and/or jury*.
7. *Conclusions* are made by the judge and/or jury based on the evidence presented.

These elements explain the roles of the participants in the criminal justice system. They also create a fundamental of notebook writing. When writing notes, the officer must remember what is and what is not his or her role. The officer's role is to present precise, relevant evidence; it is not to draw conclusions. The officer's job is to prove, not conclude. The judge and/or jury are the ones who draw conclusions.

Consequently, the purpose of narrative notes is to allow the receiver an opportunity to make an informed conclusion. Abstract generalizations and paraphrasing prevent informed conclusions from being made. Precise notes are the requirement for informed conclusions.

RSP PRINCIPLES APPLIED

RSP principles, stressing relevance, precision, and structure, were explained in Chapter 5. The following explains how to apply them to narrative notes.

Facts-in-Issue

Content quality is directly proportional to relevance. What are relevant notes? Every offence is composed of facts-in-issue, referring to the key elements that form the offence. Identity of offender, place of offence, offence date, and **mens rea** (the intent to commit an offence) are the same facts-in-issue for all criminal offences. The facts-in-issue that compose the *actus reus* are different for every offence. They are determined by reading the statutory provision that defines a specific offence and identifying the key words or terms. "Relevance" refers to information that proves or relates to at least one of the facts-in-issue of the offence. The facts-in-issue are the central focus of all witness interviews and corresponding notes. In other words, you must know exactly what has to be proved to successfully lay a charge.

Content Quality

How is the quality of notes measured? It is measured by the extent to which concrete writing is used, or the extent to which abstract writing is not used. Concrete notes are excellent; abstract notes are not. The goal of notebook writing is to turn abstract words into concrete explanations. There are countless examples of abstract notes that must be replaced with concrete notes. The following are the four most common examples of turning the abstract into the concrete:

1. "Tom Joad *threatened* Gloria." The word "threatened" may be the most common abstract paraphrase and the most misused word in law enforcement. It is often wrongly associated with a wide range of behaviours that simply do not constitute the dual procedure offence of "uttering threats." It does not inform the reader about the words or conduct that constituted the offence. The words "threat," "threatening," and "threatened" are conclusions reserved for a judge. Any notes or testimony that uses only these terms, without the exact dialogue, has no evidential value; the words do not prove that the offence was committed.

   It is imperative that the writer understand the meaning of the word. A threat is a "denunciation" to a person of ill to befall him or her, especially a declaration of hostile determination or of loss, pain, punishment, or damage to be inflicted in retribution for or conditionally upon some course.[8] This means that words and/or conduct compose the offence. A proper concrete note is "Tom Joad said to Gloria 'I am going to kill you.'"

   Problems are compounded when notes combine more than one abstraction in one sentence; for example, "The suspect has *threatened* the suspect *in the past*." The "past" is turned into concrete terms by explaining the dates, times, and places.

   "The security guard saw the accused person *steal* the item." "Shoplifting," a slang term, is a common occurrence investigated by patrol officers. "Steal" is an abstract paraphrase defined in section 2 of the *Criminal Code* (CC) as meaning "to commit theft." "Theft" is another abstract word. It is defined in section 322 CC as "moving an item with the intent to steal." Turning this abstraction into concrete terms requires an explanation of the precise act, such as "The accused person walked into aisle #3. He stopped at the CD display. He picked up a CD named 'The Rising' by Bruce Springsteen. He turned his head to the left and then to the right. He put the CD inside his jacket."

2. "The driver was *impaired*." Intoxication is an abstract term. It is a fact-in-issue for some offences. It is an opinion that needs justification. The opinion must be justified by physical symptoms, which form the concrete explanation for impairment or intoxication. The concrete replacement is, "The driver had a smell of an alcoholic beverage on his breath. His eyes

were red. After he exited the car, he was unbalanced when he walked. His speech was slurred." Arguably, "unbalanced" and "slurred speech" are both abstract words. They need additional concrete explanation to answer questions, including (a) how exactly was he unbalanced and where did it occur? (b) what part of his verbal statement was slurred? (c) to what extent was it slurred? Was the speech understandable or not?

3. "Virgil became *hostile* and *aggressive*, and then *assaulted* Ike." Three abstract generalizations are in this note. "Assaulted" must be replaced with an explanation of the specific force used. For example, a concrete replacement is, "Virgil punched Ike in the face with his right fist."

    Words such as "hostile" and "aggressive" may be the worst types of abstract generalizations because they have countless, wide-ranging interpretations. We use these paraphrases for two reasons—convenience and a desire to influence. It is easier to generalize about a person's behaviour than to specify it. We instinctively try to magnify the intensity and severity of the offence that followed the behaviour by adding influential words such as hostile. Replace these abstractions with the precise conduct and statements made. "Hostile" and "aggressive" are redundant because the violent act that occurred logically implies the offender's hostility and aggression.

4. "An *attempt* was made to enter the back door. *Damage* was found at the *side door* where *forced entry* occurred." The specific method used to enter a place often becomes habitual among offenders. "Similar acts" committed by offenders are significant because they help prove identity. Break and enter notes often combine several abstract generalizations. The words "attempt," "forced," and "damage" lack precision to be meaningful evidence. Each word is a conclusion made after an observation.

    Consequently, concrete replacement notes should describe what was seen, such as (a) "a ground level window open two inches and footprints in the soil beneath the window," (b) "seven one-inch indentations on a wooden door frame, three feet above the ground," and (c) "a wooden door and the wooden frame splintered at the same level as the lock. The door was completely open. An imprint of a shoe pattern was on the door, three feet above the ground and four inches from the frame. The shoe print was a size 10 with 14 triangular patterns." "Back door" should be replaced with an explanation of the direction the door faced (e.g., south), where it was located on the place (back), number of doors on that side of the place, material structure of the door (e.g., wood, aluminum), dimensions of the door, measurements identifying location of locks and handles, surface beneath that entrance (e.g., soil, asphalt), and visibility to other places and potential witnesses.

CONCRETE FORMAL INSTRUCTIONS

The following notes are examples of possible formal instruction that may be conveyed to suspects during investigations:

- ► "I told him he was under arrest."
- ► "I informed him of the right to counsel."

- ▸ "I informed him of the reason for the arrest."
- ▸ "I cautioned him."
- ▸ "I made a demand for breath samples."
- ▸ "I made a demand for a blood sample."

The above examples are all abstract paraphrases of the actual instructions conveyed. Each instruction is composed of formal content, explained in the supplementary textbook *Criminal Investigation*. The content of most of these instructions is recorded on cards that are carried by police officers so that the information can be communicated accurately. However, there will be circumstances that prevent the convenience of reading from a printed card. In those cases, the instructions may be identical to what is printed on the card—if it was memorized accurately, or it may be different.

A common practice, to conserve time, is to paraphrase in a notebook by simply recording the name of the instruction—"The accused person was informed of the right to counsel." This is acceptable only if it was read from a card and an accompanying note is made stating that it was read from a card. If the card was not used, record verbatim what was communicated to the suspect.

During testimony, do not state the paraphrased instruction regardless of whether a card was used. Stating the paraphrase alone is insufficient evidence because it states the outcome only, which is a conclusion. Essentially, paraphrased instructions provide no evidence of what precise information was conveyed. Consequently, always testify about the verbatim instruction conveyed to the arrested person, whether or not it was given by reading a card.

SUSPECTS' VERBATIM RESPONSES

- ▸ "The accused person confessed."
- ▸ "He admitted that he did it."
- ▸ "He understood."
- ▸ "He consented."

These are examples of responses, made by an offender, that constitute significant evidence. Each is an abstract paraphrase that provides no evidence during testimony. They are conclusions reserved for a judge to make.

A confession is the best type of evidence that constitutes a *prima facie* case during a trial and that forms reasonable grounds during an investigation. Consequently, a suspect's responses during questioning may be the most important observation that has to be recorded in a notebook.

Record all verbal statements made by an offender verbatim, meaning direct word-for-word quotes. This includes **inculpatory**, **exculpatory**, and unrelated verbal statements. Additionally, your questions and comments that precede and follow the offender's responses must be recorded verbatim. Essentially, the entire dialogue is recorded verbatim, even if it is also recorded electronically.

During questioning, an offender may respond by gestures, with or without words, or by remaining silent. Any conduct, unaccompanied by words, is a statement. The best example is shrugging shoulders in response to a question. When you ask, "Why did you do this?" and the offender makes no verbal response, then precisely explain his conduct in words. If he shrugs his shoulders, simply describe that act in those words. Do not generalize by writing "He *indicated* that he didn't know" or "had no reason." The word "indicated," when used alone in this context, is meaningless.

Another example occurred during an actual interrogation of an accused person charged with break, enter, and theft into a home. In response to the question "Why did you do this?" the accused extended a forearm, placed his other hand on it, and moved the thumb of that hand up and down, simulating the injection of a needle. The incorrect notes would have been, "He indicated drugs were the reason." The correct method was to record it as explained above.

When conduct without words is a response, the worst notes possible are "No response" or "He remained silent." This will eliminate valuable evidence. These notes must be made only when the suspect is silent and exhibits no conduct in response to your question or comment.

Confessions are not only made to police officers; they are made to citizens. The same notebook rules apply when recording a confession made to any person other than a police officer.

Obtaining consent is an integral part of an investigation. It is relevant to several police procedures including questioning, searching, and voluntary accompaniment (when circumstances do not authorize arrest or detention). When a suspect consents, do not simply record "He consented." This type of note states only a conclusion. Record his response verbatim. A refusal to comply with a demand for a breath or blood sample during an impaired driving investigation must be recorded verbatim. Refusal to comply with these demands constitutes an offence. Do not write an abstract note of "He refused." Instead, replace it with the verbatim response representing concrete evidence.

The prosecution has the burden of proving that all instructions and demands are understood by the accused. Proving the accused person's knowledge is accomplished by recording the response verbatim. Do not write, "The accused understood the [specific information]." This type of testimony has no evidential value; once again, it is a conclusion reserved for a trial judge to make.

Factors Affecting Observation

The circumstances associated with observations, and the ability to explain them, prove the level of credibility of the observation. A number of factors affect credibility evaluation; they are explained in Chapter 9 of the supplemental textbook, *Criminal Investigation*. These factors relate to events that occur before, during, and after an offence. Some of these factors include:

- intent to learn;
- position;
- duration of the observation;
- time of note taking; and
- activity between observation and notebook recording.

Explaining these factors precisely is the difference between mediocre and excellent notes.

The following are examples of how to apply this principle:

- *Intent to learn*: The intent to learn refers to an awareness that an offence might occur. Knowledge of circumstances creates an awareness that an observation of a crime may be made. Determining the presence or absence of the intent to learn is important for analyzing the extent of the observation. Consequently, record your activity, and particularly the area of attention or focus, before the offence occurred. Include what was seen or heard prior to the crime.

- *Position*: This is sometimes forgotten because of the emphasis on remembering the observation. We get caught up with trying to remember the details of what happened, causing us to neglect recording where we were when the observation was made. The distance between the observer and the occurrence must be recorded for accurate credibility evaluation. The observer's position during a crime may not always be stationary; it may change during the offence. The best example is impaired driving. Usually, the officer is mobile when observing this offence. The distance between the officer and the offender may change. Notes must reflect whether the distance changed or remained the same throughout the observation. Describe the nature of the view, including the presence or absence of obstructions and the degree of illumination.

- *Duration of observation*: According to the Supreme Court of Canada in *R v. Nikolovski* (1996),[9] "duration of observation" is a genuine factor that requires assessment to determine credibility of an observation. Record the estimated length of time that a person or vehicle is observed during a relevant event pertaining to an offence.

- *Time of note taking*: Record the time when the notes were made. This notation will be required for a judge to conclude whether notes were made as soon as possible after the observation, which is the principal determinant about whether a notebook can be used during court testimony to refresh memory. Do not simply record that the notes were made "as soon as possible" afterward. This note will have no value to the judge's assessment.

- *Activity between observation and notebook recording*: What you do between an observation and the time that you record relevant notes is vital to determine whether any significant activity obstructed or interfered with recall at the time the notes were written. Consequently, record your activity between those two times. If nothing significant occurred, note the absence of any mental interference. For example, if your observation included a vehicle plate number, then dialing a telephone or remembering other numbers, this may be relevant to the recall accuracy at the time the notes were made. If such activity did not occur, it should be noted to refresh memory during court testimony to help prove the credibility of the observation.

Systematic Descriptions

Descriptions of persons and items can be structured efficiently by dividing a description into two categories:

1. general features; and
2. specific features.

General features refer to characteristics that are not unique. General features, alone, are insufficient for positive identification. Conversely, specific features are unique to that person or item. Alone, or in conjunction with general features, they allow the person or item to be positively identified or recognized.

Descriptions should begin with general features followed by specific ones, forming a suitable structure that facilitates recall and comprehension by a reader.

General features include:

Person
- Gender/race
- Height
- Weight
- Build
- Hair colour, length
- Eye colour

Item
- Make
- Model
- Type
- Colour
- Size

Specific features include

Person
- Scars
- Tattoos
- Clothes, jewelry in conjunction with general description
- Unique features that create uncommon appearance, such as a hairstyle

Item
- Damage
- Wear marks
- Serial number (VIN for cars)
- Additions to the item after manufacture, such as stickers, writing, or print

Crime Scene Protection

The objectives and procedures relevant to crime scene protection are explained in Chapter 4 of the supplementary textbook, *Criminal Investigation*. The first officer's notes must include a precise description of the crime scene's physical appearance upon his or her arrival. The location of a crime scene varies significantly. It may be inside a house, business, or vehicle, or it may be outside in a private or public place. A combination of written description and a rough diagram must explain the entire appearance, including (a) entrances; (b) positions of furniture, weapons, physical evidence, injured or deceased persons; (c) lights that were on or off; (d) appliances that were on or off, including volume levels; (e) entrance and exit routes used by the offender(s); (f) times of entry and departure of authorized personnel, including the routes used by them; and (g) any alteration to the crime scene that occurred prior to photographing and expert analysis by forensic officers.

Justify Opinions

Generally, opinions are a form of evidence that is inadmissible in court. However, some opinions are exempt from that rule and are admissible. A complete explanation is found in the accompanying textbook, *Criminal Investigation*. Some common examples of admissible opinions include:

- intoxication;
- distance;
- speed; and
- facial recognition.

These exceptions are not automatically admissible. Justification for the opinion is needed to ensure admissibility. Use the following guidelines to justify an opinion.

- An opinion of intoxication or impairment is justified by recording the specific physical symptoms observed such as imbalance, bloodshot eyes, slurred speech, and smell of alcohol on breath.
- Facial recognition is justified by explaining the description or the circumstances that created familiarity with that person.
- An opinion of speed requires only a generalization. It can be explained as an "excessive" speed and stating a range that the speed could have been between. Additionally, a comparison may be explained in relation to other traffic.
- Distance may simply be noted by an estimated numerical figure.

Apply General Principles to Content

SUSPECTS' VERBATIM CONVERSATION

Conversation with suspects and accused persons must be recorded verbatim. This rule does not apply to complainants and witnesses whose observations are recorded in Witness Statements—a completely different report form.

There are three general environments where conversations with suspects/accused persons occur:

1. at a police station, with electronic recording equipment available and used;
2. at a police station, with no electronic recording available or practicable; and
3. in any place other than a police station where electronic recording is unavailable and impracticable.

When a formal interrogation is electronically recorded, the recording will be the obvious accurate recall source; essentially, the notes become a transcript of the recording.

Formal interrogation at a police station without electronic recording availability requires rough notes during the questioning, as explained in the supplemental textbook, *Criminal Investigation*; the verbatim conversation is not written directly into the notebook. The rough notes are retained for court.

Uniform patrol officers most commonly engage in informal questioning or dialogue at the place of arrest until arrival at the police station where the accused person is searched, booked, and then lodged in a cell. There are countless circumstances that accompany a conversation with an offender. They include:

- responding to a call of an offence "in progress," finding an offender committing an offence, making an arrest, and transporting him to a police station;
- making an arrest at the conclusion of an investigation (after an offender has left the crime scene); and
- during the preliminary stage of an investigation when a potential suspect is questioned and only mere suspicion exists to believe that the suspect committed an offence.

These three situational examples all demand attention to officer safety, and each has considerable stress, albeit in varying degrees. These factors will prevent rough notes; consequently, conversations will be recorded from memory recall.

The format for recording sequenced verbatim conversation is as follows.

1. Precede or introduce all relevant conversation with the phrase, "The following conversation occurred:".
2. Write the initials of the speaker on the left side of the margin.
3. On the right side of the margin, write that speaker's direct quote.
4. On the next line write the responding speaker's initials on the left side of the margin followed by his or her direct quote on the corresponding line to the right of that margin.
5. Repeat the above steps, forming a structured, line-by-line dialogue composed of the speaker's initials followed by his or her corresponding direct quote.

EXAMPLE

The following notes were made from an actual robbery investigation where the offender entered a corner store, assaulted a 17-year-old female employee, and stole $15.00. One day later, an informant provided the following information. The offender met him in a bar less than ten minutes after the robbery, told him that he committed the offence, and showed him the $15.00 that was stolen. There are three participants in the conversation:

1. G.A. (police officer #1),
2. C.P. (police officer #2), and
3. R.R. (accused person).

NOTES
▶ format for direct quotes

▶ precise instruction instead of paraphrasing

19:12	10-7: 3001 Creighton St.
	Knocked on side door. Male person answered. The followed conversation occurred.
G.A.:	I'm Cst. (Surname). This is Cst. (Surname). We're with the ————— Regional Police. Can we come in?
R.R.:	(motioned with hand to enter)
G.A.:	Are you (accused's name—R.R.)?
R.R.:	Ya.
G.A.:	You're under arrest for the robbery at 556 Queen's St., the Avondale Store, last night.
R.R.:	What? I was with my girlfriend.
G.A.:	It is my duty to inform you that you have the right to retain and instruct counsel without delay. Do you understand?
R.R.:	Ya.
G.A.:	It means you can call a lawyer of your choice. Do you understand?
R.R.:	Ya.
19:24	10-7 33 Division
	— escorted R.R. to booking room
	— searched again
	— led to 2nd floor interrogation room
	— no conversation
19:27	Interrogation began

G.A.:	Is there any reason why you robbed the store?
R.R.:	I didn't. I don't know what you're talking about.
G.A.:	It's not a question of if you did it, but why you did it. Was it for money?
R.R.:	(no response)
G.A.:	There's got to be a reason for you to rob a store and grab the girl. Were you short of cash?
R.R.:	I don't know anything about this.
G.A.:	Listen, we've gone through this. There's no question you did it. There's got to be a reason for you to do this.
R.R.:	(no response)
G.A.:	This is more serious than a simple shoplifting. Why would you grab the girl too? Why would you do something like this?

R.R.:	(he extended his right hand and rubbed his thumb and fingers) "CASH."
O.A.:	Are you that bad off?
R.R.:	(nodded his head)
O.A.:	What about welfare or something like that?
R.R.:	There's problems at my house. My dad hasn't worked in five years. What's welfare worth? You can't even buy a pair of jeans.
O.A.:	But at least it's something.
R.R.:	But there's more to it.
O.A.:	Are you working?
R.R.:	I was, just part time. I was working at some subdivision doing drywalling. I couldn't believe it the next day that I did this. I've never done anything like this before. She's not hurt bad is she?
O.A.:	No.
R.R.:	But, all I did was shove her away. I can't believe I did it.
O.A.:	She says there's marks on her neck and that you grabbed her hair.
R.R.:	I shoved her. I reached in the till and she grabbed the till or something and I shoved her down. Boy, I feel like crying right now.
O.A.:	Are you going to give us a written statement?
R.R.:	Sure, I've never done anything like this before. I drank a lot that day. I got to straighten out.
20:11	Statement commenced.
20:18	Statement complete.
	— escorted to cell area and lodged in cell #3
20:23	— wrote notes
20:51	— 10-6 reports

RSP Principles Applied to Common Occurrences

The following are examples of common offences that uniform patrol officers investigate. Each example is intended to show how to replace paraphrasing with precise observations.

DISTURBANCE

One of the most routine calls for service is a disturbance in a public place such as a bar. "Cause a disturbance" is a summary conviction *Criminal Code* offence. The word "disturbance" is an outcome or conclusion made by a judge. The precise behaviours that constitute a disturbance include shouting, swearing, fighting, using obscene language, and being drunk. Consequently, the word "disturbance" is a paraphrase. It should not be used exclusively to describe the observation. Instead, precisely explain the behaviour.

22:26	10-7 Bottoms Up Bar, 3001 Creighton St.
	Re: disturbance
	Entered via front door. Approximately 30 patrons inside. An employee
	pointed to the bar and pointed to a man who they wanted removed. From
	a distance of about 10 metres, I saw a man, white, about 25 years, 5'8",
	190 lbs, short dark hair wearing a black "T-shirt with a red "X" on the
	front, shouting at the bartender, "Give me another beer, I want more beer."
	As I walked toward him, I saw that he was unbalanced and he staggered
	as he walked two steps toward the bar. His words were slightly slurred
	and he yelled again, "Hey you, I said I want more beer." As I approached
	him, I saw that he had red eyes and I smelled an alcoholic beverage on his
	breath as I stood in front of him. He screamed again at the bartender,
	"Hey you (insert actual obscenities), give me another (actual obscenity)
	beer." Several people were looking at him. I said to him, "Come with me,
	you have to leave." This man screamed, "(insert actual obscenity) off, pig."
22.18	I told him, "You're under arrest for causing a disturbance." I took hold of
	his left arm and escorted him outside. He said nothing. We arrived at my
	cruiser. I searched him and seated him in the back seat.

The notebook would continue with verbatim conversation, including formal instructions given to the accused person and personal information elicited from him.

IMPAIRED DRIVING

Investigations and prosecutions of drinking and driving offences are largely predicated on police officers' observations. The supplemental textbook *Impaired Driving Investigations* explains the procedural complexities of the relevant offences and how to investigate them. The following example shows how to apply the principles previously explained in this chapter to impaired driving investigations. Additionally, it incorporates the need for precise descriptions of physical symptoms and verbatim conversation.

00:34	I was stopped at a red light on Hec St. at Creighton St., facing north. I was
	the first car in line. I saw a blue Intrepid travelling east on Creighton St. It
	was about 30 metres from the intersection. The vehicle turned right onto
	Hec St. at an excessive rate of speed. The right turn was excessively wide.
	The vehicle travelled onto the southbound lane, about 3 metres east of the
	mid-point of the roadway. As the car turned right, I saw a male person,

	about 35 yrs, driving. I saw no other occupants. I was about 5 metres
	away from the Intrepid when I saw the driver. After the car completed the
	right turn, I activated the roof lights and siren and drove through the
	intersection while the northbound traffic light was red. I accelerated to
	60 km/h to reach a distance of about 10 metres behind the Intrepid. I read
	the back plate—Ontario XMEN4.
00:38	I followed the Intrepid at 65 km/h for about .5 km. From Regent St. to
	Division St., half of the car was on the southbound lane. The car abruptly
	slowed down and turned sharply to the right curb.
	The vehicle stopped at a 30 degree angle from the curb. I stopped about
	5 metres behind the car. I got out of the cruiser and walked to the driver's
	door. I stood slightly behind the driver's door and leaned close to the open
	window. The car was running. The driver was male/white, about 35 years,
	short blonde hair, clean shaven, wearing a black T-shirt with a large red
	"X" printed on the front, and blue jeans. I smelled a strong odour of alcohol
	on his breath. His eyes were not fully open and were red/bloodshot. The
	following conversation occurred:
G.A.:	Can I see your driver's licence?
B.G.:	(searched his pockets and front seat)
	(opened his wallet and passed his licence twice without removing it).
G.A.:	How much have you had to drink?
B.G.:	A few (slurred) ah, not much (slurred), a few.
	— I opened the driver's door and took hold of his left arm.
G.A.:	You have to get out of the car.
	— He had poor coordination. He tripped by hitting his left foot as he exited.
00:41	after he exited, I held him by his left arm.
G.A.:	You're under arrest for impaired driving. Let's go to my cruiser.
	— I escorted him to my cruiser, searched him, and seated him in the back.
	— I returned to his car and turned off the ignition.

The remainder of the notes would explain the formal instructions, accused person's responses, and other relevant procedures associated to impaired driving investigations.

Belated Offence—Hearsay Evidence

The majority of notes written will be to explain belated offences, those that occurred in the past and the offender departed before police arrival. Notes regarding belated offences will largely be **hearsay evidence.** Hearsay is generally inadmissible during court testimony. Hearsay notes are needed primarily to write the GOR. Although the study of rules of evidence is beyond the scope of this textbook (it is explained in the

Criminal Investigation textbook), the following is an example of how to distinguish hearsay notes from admissible personal observations in relation to a common belated offence:

Hearsay	19:10	10-7 3001 Queen St.
		Re: break, enter, and theft
		Complainant: Hec Creighton
		Address: same
		D.O.B.: 30-01-02
		Phone: (404) 240-3001
		Mr. Creighton is the owner of the house. He left for work at 07:45 hrs today and he locked all the doors. Returned home at 19:00 hrs.
Admissible personal observations (perceived by own senses)		Point of entry: back door (south side). Inside wooden door was open. The door and frame were splintered. Wood fragments were on the floor, inside that entrance. Seven dents were on the door near the doorknob, about 2 m from the ground.
Hearsay		Only item stolen:
		20" Sony TV—silver and black
		— serial number 04-3001-2002
		— volume button missing
		— value: $500.00
		— stolen from living room
		— nothing else touched or moved
	19:45	10-8

CONTENT

Content refers to the actual information acquired during an investigation. It refers to the *evidence* emerging from the observations of others or personal observations. The content recorded in your notebook will be the same content written in reports and conveyed during testimony. The content follows a path; the starting point is the notebook. The quality of reports and testimony depends on the quality of notebook content.

The only difference between notebook content and report content or testimony is formality. Usually, notebook content is written as informal rough notes, representing the starting point of the content path. The informal rough notes are then converted into formal written and verbal communication.

Notebook content is divided into two groups:

1. cover page information, and
2. narrative information.

The cover page of a GOR or arrest report is a one-page, fill-in-the-blank document. A wide range of information is needed to describe the relevant persons, places, times, and items. See Chapter 7, page 60, for an example of a blank cover page. It illustrates the information you need to record in your notebook in order to complete this page.

Narrative information refers to a comprehensive story. It is the most important part of a report; it requires skill, as opposed to simply filling in blanks. Each narrative will be unique because every investigation has distinctive elements. However, a generic template can guide a narrative.

Memory

"Contemporaneous notes" are rough notes written by you as soon as is practical after the observation. What is the primary significance of contemporaneous notes? Memory decay. Every human suffers from memory decay.

Front-line policing involves *information overload*. It is impossible to accurately remember all relevant details learned and acquired during every tour of duty; the volume of information is overwhelming. Memory recall is needed at various times. **Short-term recall** is needed to remember information for reports. **Long-term recall** is needed for court testimony.

Research shows that police training does not necessarily improve accuracy of memory recall and that police officers cannot hold more information in memory systems than citizens do.[10] Paying attention and *conscious review* (repeated thinking about an observation) are two ways to improve memory. The third way is to preserve the observation by recording it as soon as is practical after the observation is made. The importance of preventing unjustified delays in writing notes is illustrated by **Ebbinghaus's Forgetting Curve**.

Ebbinghaus's Forgetting Curve

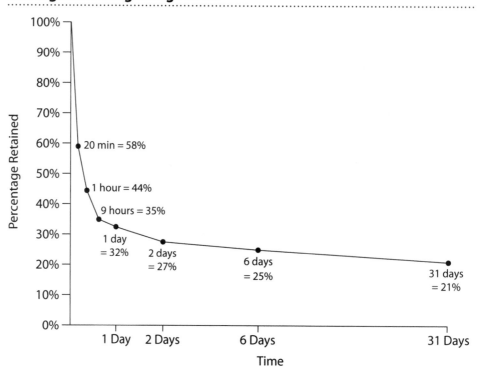

Hermann Ebbinghaus, a pioneer of scientific memory research, published the first significant memory study in 1885. It was centrally focused on memory retention and the rate of forgetting. Ebbinghaus concluded that:

- 58 percent of new information is retained after 20 minutes. This means that almost half of new information is forgotten within 20 minutes of acquiring it.
- 44 percent of new information is retained after one hour, meaning more than half is forgotten after one hour expires.
- 25 percent of new information is retained after six days, meaning that three-quarters is forgotten in less than one week.
- After six days, the rapid rate of forgetting declines. Between 6 days and 31 days, only 4 percent more information is forgotten. In other words, about the same amount of information is remembered between one and four weeks—only one-quarter of the new information.

Conscious review, through studying, rehearsing, or thinking about the new information, dramatically slows the rate of forgetting and increases retention, causing an incline toward 100 percent recall. Afterward, forgetting again occurs but conscious review will reverse the decline. Consequently, repeated conscious review drastically alters Ebbinghaus's Forgetting Curve by retention of between 75 and 100 percent of the new information.[11]

Ebbinghaus's Forgetting Curve—Change in Retention with Conscious Review

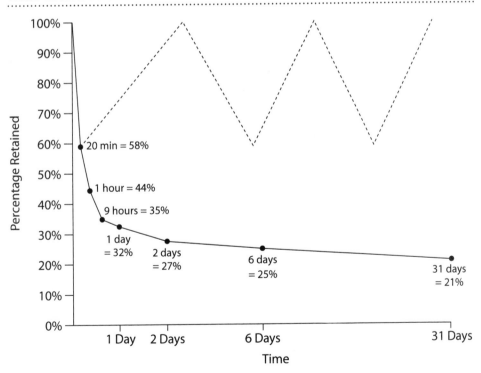

LEGAL SIGNIFICANCE

The Supreme Court of Canada (SCC) has cautioned us about the problems associated with memory decay and the need for all witnesses, both police and citizens, to use means of refreshing memory. In *R v. Coffin* (1956),[12] the SCC identified time lapse and stress as contributing factors to forgetfulness. In *R v. Fliss* (2002),[13] the SCC recognized that even individuals "blessed with prodigious memory" will not have total recall of lengthy conversations with accused persons without the assistance of some aid that refreshes memory. According to the SCC, "common sense would say" that some observations may remain in one's memory forever if the circumstances are unique or distinct, but that most observations will not be fully recalled without some assistance.

Common sense therefore implies that extremely unique, distinct observations may remain in long-term memory for a lifetime, but most observations, including the rare unique observations, cannot be fully recalled without the assistance of recorded notes.[14]

In summary, contemporaneous notes are expected. You need to refresh your memory with written notes and need to refer to those notes in order to ensure accurate recall.

NOTES

1. *Municipal Freedom of Information and Protection of Privacy Act*, RSO 1990, c. M.56.
2. Ibid., section 8(1).
3. Ibid., section 2(1), definition of "personal information."
4. http://www.ipc.on.ca/images/Resources/up-durham_e.pdf.
5. *R v. Barrett* (1993), 82 CCC (3d) 266 (Ont. CA).
6. *Archibald v. The Queen* (1956), 116 CCC (Que. SC).
7. *R v. Khan* (1990), 59 CCC (3d) 92 (SCC).
8. *R v. Ross* (1986), 26 CCC (3d) 413 (Ont. CA).
9. *R v. Nikolovski* (1996), 111 CCC (3d) 403 (SCC).
10. Yarmey, A.D. (1986). Perceived expertness and credibility of police officers as eyewitnesses. *Canadian Police Journal* 10(1): 31-52.
11. Ebbinghaus, H. (1885). *Memory: A Contribution to Experimental Psychology.* Reprint. New York: Dover, 1963.
12. *R v. Coffin* (1956).
13. *R v. Fliss*, [2002] 1 SCR 535, 2002 SCC 16.
14. Ibid.

CHAPTER 7
General Occurrence Report

PURPOSE

A General Occurrence Report (GOR) is the most common type of police report. It is a written record of any incident (except a motor vehicle collision) requiring any extent of police investigation, assistance, or response where no arrest has yet been made or will be made. When an investigation results in custody, a GOR converts to, or is replaced by, an Arrest Report.

The distinguishing features of a GOR are as follows.

- The topics covered by a GOR include offences (criminal and provincial) and occurrences where no offence has been committed (e.g., missing person, sudden death involving no criminal act).
- A GOR explains the extent of an investigation until the investigation is complete. This means that the length of a GOR varies.
- A GOR justifies past and future investigative acts. This means that the GOR conveys a belief (e.g., mere suspicion, reasonable grounds).

GORs are composed of:

1. a cover page, and
2. a narrative.

Cover Page

A cover page is a simple fill-in-the-blank document that requires no special skill except OR (offence/occurrence recognition) to fill in the box with the heading "Type of Incident." Accurate OR gives a GOR a title and a focus for its narrative.

The cover page introduces the reader to the participants, places, times, and items involved in the incident. In some cases, the box may be of insufficient size to include the relevant information; write "Refer to narrative" if this is the case. When the complainant is a place instead of a person, write "I" (for "Institution") in the "Sex" box instead of "Male" or "Female."

General Incident ☐ **Arrest Report** ☐

Request for Summons ☐
NO. OF SUPPLEMENTARY REPORTS

YOUNG OFFENDER ☐

DESCRIPTION OF PROPERTIES OR INJURIES(IMC.SERIAL NOS.) | VALUE | DAMAGED | RECOVERED

INJURIES: MAJOR ☐ MINOR ☐ NONE ☐

SPECIFY ON SUPPLEMENTARY: TYPE OF INJURIES SUSTAINED, TYPE OF FORCED USED.
SUFFICIENT DETAILS FOR PLEA OF GUILTY. CO-ACCUSED, PREVIOUS ADDRESS OF ACCUSED, ETC.

FOR NARRATIVE COMPLETE SUPPLEMENTARY REPORT

DATE & TIME OF ARREST | ARRESTING OFFICER

LOCATION OF ARREST | HAZARD ☐

CHARGES(IF WARRANT EXECUTED, STATE TYPE)

CHARGES

NOTIFICATIONS: Y.O.A. - NOTICE TO PARENT SERVED ☐ YES ☐ NO

OTHERS: ☐ SPOUSE ☐ GUARDIAN ☐ OTHER - NAME:
☐ PARENT ☐ NEXT OF KIN

ADDRESS | HOME PHONE

ARRESTED FOR OTHER DEPT. (NAME) | WHO NOTIFIED? | TIME

RELEASED TO (NAME/RANK/No.) | TIME | YR. | MO. | DAY

FINGERPRINT DATE | FORM OF RELEASE | BAIL HEARING YES ☐ NO ☐

BAIL & RELEASE RECOMMENDATIONS | STATEMENT TAKEN YES ☐ NO ☐

CNI/CPIC QUERIED? RESULTS

RELEASED BY OFFICER | NAME J.P.

DATE & TIME OF RELEASE | COURT | COURT DATE & TIME

HAZARD REMARKS (MUST BE COMPLETED IF HAZARD CHECKED)

STATS. CANADA | CLEARED BY | INCIDENT CLASS | ADULTS M F | JUVENILES M F | INF.
CHARGE | OTHER | UNF. | | | | DATE CLEARED

OFFICE ONLY | DATA ENTRY | DATA VERIF. | DATA RECEIVED IN RECORDS

DIVISION | PATROL AREA/ZONE | INCIDENT CLASS | INCIDENT NO.

TYPE OF INCIDENT | TIME & DATE OF INCIDENT (TIME OR BETWEEN) | YR. | MO. | DAY | HAZARD ☐

LOCATION OF INCIDENT

HOW INCIDENT COMMITTED | MEANS (WEAPONS, TOOLS USED)

VICTIM / COMPLAINANT

SURNAME | GIVEN(1) | GIVEN(2) | RACE | WHITE ☐ NON-WHITE ☐

ADDRESS | HOME PHONE | HAZARD ☐

SEX | YR. | DOB MO. | DAY | MAR. ST. | OCCUPATION | CONDITION Sober ☐ Intox ☐ | HBD ☐ Drugs ☐

PLACE OF EMPLOYMENT/EMPLOYER | BUSINESS PHONE | (EXT. /LOCAL)

REPORTED BY

SURNAME | GIVEN(1) | GIVEN(2) | GIVEN(3)

ADDRESS | HAZARD ☐

SEX | YR. | DOB MO. | DAY | RELATIONSHIP TO VICTIM/COMPLAINANT | CONDITION Sober ☐ Intox ☐ | HBD ☐ Drugs ☐

PLACE OF EMPLOYMENT/EMPLOYER | BUSINESS PHONE | (EXT. /LOCAL)

VEH.USED

TYPE | LICENCE No. | LIC.YR. | LIC. PROV. | VEH.YR. | MAKE | MODEL

STYLE | COLOUR | VIN

OWNER SAME ☐

OUTSTANDING FEATURES

ACCUSED / SUSPECT.

SURNAME | GIVEN(1) | GIVEN(2) | NICK NAMES | ALIAS ☐ NEE ☐

ADDRESS | HOME PHONE | HAZARD ☐

SEX | YR. | DOB MO. | DAY | AGE | MAR.ST. | MHT(HT) | MASS(WT) | RACE | WHITE ☐ NON-WHITE ☐

HAIR COLOUR | MOUSTACHE ☐ BEARD ☐ WIG ☐ | EYES-COLOUR | ☐ CONTACT LENS ☐ GLASSES | DESCRIPTION OF CLOTHING

BUILD | HAIR TYPE | COMPLEXION | TEETH
☐ SLENDER ☐ BALD ☐ CURLY/WAVY | ☐ SALLOW | ☐ GOOD | ☐ PROTRUD. UPPERS
☐ MEDIUM ☐ PART BALD ☐ WELL DRESSED | ☐ LIGHT/FAIR | ☐ IRREGULAR | ☐ PROTRUD. LOWERS
☐ HEAVY ☐ SHORT ☐ UNKEMPT | ☐ RUDDY | ☐ FALSE | ☐ VISIBLE DECAY
☐ LONG ☐ BUSHY | ☐ FRECKLED | ☐ VISIBLE GOLD | ☐ VISIBLE MISSING
☐ STRAIGHT | ☐ DARK/SWARTHY | ☐ STAINED
| ☐ POCK-MARKED

VICTIM/ACCUSED RELATIONSHIP | DRIVER'S LICENCE No. | PROV. | N.R.P. No.

PHYSICAL/MENTAL CONDITION, MARKS, SCARS, TATTOOS, OUTSTANDING FEATURES | F.P.S. No.

CNI CAUTION | V ☐ E ☐ A ☐ | CONDITION Sober ☐ Intox ☐ | HBD ☐ Drugs ☐ | OCCUPATION
| M ☐ S ☐ C ☐

PLACE OF EMPLOYMENT/EMPLOYER/SCHOOL/ GRADE | BUS. PHONE | (EXT. /LOCAL)

REPORTING OFFICER (FULL NAME/RANK/ NO.) | DATE/TIME REPORT TAKEN | YR. | MO. | DAY | TIME

OTHER OFFICER(S) ATTENDING | I.D. OFFICER RESPONDING

REPORT CHECKED BY (FULL NAME/RANK/NO.) | CASE REASSIGNED TO | BY | DATE

REPORT CHECKED BY (FULL NAME/RANK/NO.) | INCIDENT STATUS(IF INVEST.COMP.CHECK SOLVED OR UNSOLVED)
INVEST. CONT. ☐ INVEST. COMP. ☐ SOLVED ☐ UNSOLVED ☐ | INIT./DATE

Narrative

A narrative is a relevant, structured, precise (RSP) story that recreates the occurrence and investigation. It is written in a document called a "Supplementary Report," referring to lined paper with condensed boxes corresponding to the cover page.

Every narrative, regardless of severity of occurrence, is guided by the RSP system. In other words, the RSP system *customizes* any narrative from simple to complex.

OCCURRENCE CLASSIFICATION

There are four classifications of investigations that apply to GORs:

1. belated–reactive
2. belated–proactive
3. in progress–reactive
4. in progress–proactive

There are two *sources* of calls for service, referring to how the call originates:

1. proactive—a police office finds an occurrence being committed; and
2. reactive—a citizen calls the police, an officer **R**eacts and **R**esponds, and the citizen **R**eports an occurrence to the police.

There are two *time relationships* between the source of the call and the actual commission of the occurrence:

1. in progress, and
2. belated (not in progress).

"In-progress" calls are more complex and dangerous because of the greater risk and uncertainty involved. These emergencies often include the *presence* of offenders, injured victims, and physical evidence. Belated calls have greater time separating the offence and police response. The *absence* of offenders and injured persons reduces the initial risk, but the delay between call and offence increases the challenge of identifying and finding offenders.

The belated–reactive call is the most common of the four classifications and the easiest to learn. Consequently, it will be used as the starting point for learning how to write a GOR narrative.

Occurrence Status

Every GOR narrative explains an investigation. Every investigation has a status— "open" or "closed." *Open* means unsolved; *closed* means solved.

An open investigation is communicated by the phrase "investigation continues." A closed investigation is communicated by the word "cleared," followed by one of the following three terms:

1. by charge (the offence has been solved by **laying an Information**, the document used to charge an adult or young offender);
2. otherwise (reasonable grounds exist that proves who the offender is but the offence is solved by *not* laying an Information; the solution is a means other than charging the offender); or

Supplementary Report

CHECK APPROPRIATE BOX

ORIGINAL ☐   MISSING PERSON/ELOPEE ☐
ARREST ☐   FRAUDULENT DOCUMENT ☐
INCIDENT ☐   HOMICIDE/SUDDEN DEATH ☐
VEHICLE ☐   OTHER ☐

DIVISION	PATROL AREA/ZONE	INCIDENT CLASS	REFERENCE	INCIDENT No.

REFERENCE: VICTIM/COMPLAINANT   POLICE INFORMATION ☐   ACCUSED ☐

TYPE OF INCIDENT

DATE OF ORIGINAL REPORT

BUS. PHONE (EXT./LOCAL)   HOME PHONE (EXT./LOCAL)

SURNAME(OR NAME & TYPE OF BUSINESS)

ADDRESS   HAZARD ☐

REPORTING OFFICER (FULL NAME/RANK/No.)

OTHER OFFICER(S) ATTENDING

REPORT CHECKED BY (FULL NAME/RANK/No.)

REPORT CHECKED BY (FULL NAME/RANK/No.)

DATE/TIME OF THIS REPORT	YR.	MO.	DAY	TIME

I.D. OFFICER REPORTING

CASE REASSIGNED TO   BY   DATE

INCIDENT STATUS (IF INVEST. COMP. CHECK SOLVED OR UNSOLVED)
INVEST. CONT. ☐   INVEST. COMP. ☐   SOLVED ☐   UNSOLVED ☐   INIT./DATE

PAGE No.

HAZARD REMARKS (MUST BE COMPLETED IF HAZARD CHECKED)

STATS. CAN CLEARED BY	CHG.	OTHER	UNF.	INCIDENT CLASS	ADULTS M F	JUVENILES M F	INF.
OFFICE USE ONLY	DATA ENTRY	DATA VERIF.		DATA RECEIVED IN RECORDS	DATE CLEARED		

3. unfounded (the offence did not happen; some part of the offence—e.g., *mens rea*—did not occur, or the entire offence did not happen—e.g., Public Mischief—intentional fabrication).

The title of the GOR has to correspond with a status. The last line of every narrative must convey how the occurrence was "cleared." Two clearances ("by charge" and "otherwise") require forming reasonable grounds that the offence did occur and who exactly committed it. "Unfounded" requires reasonable grounds that the offence did not occur.

In summary, the status corresponds to belief (amount of evidence). The status conveys the extent of evidence obtained and whether reasonable grounds have been formed to reach a conclusion.

NARRATIVE CONCEPTS

A concept is a general procedural rule. There are six narrative concepts that provide a general guideline for writing a GOR.

1. Write in the Third Person

The writer has two choices about how to refer to himself or herself—first person or third person.

▸ First person is "I."
▸ Third person includes "police," "writer," or "Cst. (Surname)."

"I arrived" and "I interviewed" represent first-person writing. "Writer interviewed" and "police arrived" represent third-person writing.

There is no legal rule that governs which one to use. There is no law that mandates first person or third person. However, an informal survey of front-line police officers in 2007 revealed the following:

▸ most police services allow discretion about which method to use; and
▸ 100 percent of officers surveyed use, and strongly recommended, third-person writing.

First-person writing is generally regarded as elementary or juvenile, except when used in witness statements. Third-person writing is considered to represent a post-secondary level of writing, and demonstrates professionalism.

2. Use the Past Tense

The narrative explains events that occurred in the past. Therefore, use the past tense to explain an event. Exceptions are when explaining present and future risk (e.g., repetition of offence) or to describe a condition that justifies a corresponding *current* belief.

3. Use the Active Voice

Every act or conduct has four elements divided into two groups:

1. PAC (**P**erson, **A**ct/**C**onduct)—*who* did *what*
2. TP (**T**ime, **P**lace)—*where* and *when*

Narratives usually involve multiple persons and multiple acts or conducts. Your goal is to match the person with the act or conduct.

The best way to record PAC is to remember the sequence of the letters: P (who) → A/C (what). You use active voice by identifying the person first and the act/conduct second. Passive voice is opposite—describing the act/conduct first and the person second.

The active voice is most effective for two reasons.

1. It creates the correct mental image for the reader's benefit. The reader needs to visualize the person first; visualizing the act/conduct first and then attaching a person to it is confusing.
2. It eliminates the embarrassing mistake of neglecting to identify the person. Using the passive voice often causes the writer to omit the person.

EXAMPLES

Active Voice	Passive Voice
Cst. H. Creighton questioned Bill Matto.	Bill Matto was questioned. *or* Bill Matto was questioned by Cst. H. Creighton.
Cst. H. Creighton searched the car.	The car was searched. *or* The car was searched by Cst. H. Creighton.
Cst. H. Creighton found the handgun under the front seat.	The handgun was found. *or* The handgun was found by Cst. H. Creighton.
Cst. H. Creighton arrested Bill Matto.	The decision was made to arrest Bill Matto. *or* Bill Matto was arrested by Cst. H. Creighton.

Adding TP after PAC achieves clarity and credibility.

4. Write Complete, Clear Sentences

Readers will be confused by incomplete sentences and "wordy" sentences—those that include meaningless words or too many ideas. Your goal is to convey *maximum information* with *minimum words*.

Four simple rules will help you consistently write complete, clear sentences.

1. *Every complete sentence consists of two elements: a subject and a predicate.* The *subject* is the topic (what/whom the sentence is about). The *predicate* provides information about the subject; in other words, the predicate tells

the reader something about the subject. For example, "The accused person was intoxicated" is a complete sentence. "The accused person" is the subject or the topic; "was intoxicated" is the predicate.

A subject and a verb are needed to form a complete sentence. If both exist, a sentence has been formed, regardless of how simple or complex the sentence is. For example:

- "Ike drank six beers."
- "While Ike was at Bottoms Up Bar, he drank six beers between 20:00 and 22:30 hrs."

Both sentences have the same subject (Ike) and the same verb (drank).

2. *Every sentence has a basic statement or one essential meaning.*
   In the above examples, the basic statement is "Ike drank." That is the essential meaning that is being conveyed.

3. *Expand the sentence only with information relevant to the basic statement.*
   Do not include words, phrases, or any information that is irrelevant to the essential meaning of the sentence. This requires focus. Focus on the basic statement only; keep relevant information and discard the immaterial.

4. *Do not try to incorporate a second idea into one sentence.*
   Sentences with more than one essential meaning are not only excessive, they are confusing. Separate basic statements and essential meanings into distinct sentences.

5. Write Complete, Clear Paragraphs

The lack of proper paragraphs is one of the most common problems in report writing. "When do I start a new paragraph?" is a question frequently asked by students.

The following general rules will help you write complete, clear paragraphs.

1. *Follow paragraph structure.*
   What is a paragraph? The following points will assist you in writing complete, clear paragraphs.

   - All paragraphs begin with an indentation.
   - Paragraphs vary in length.
   - A paragraph is a group of sentences linked together by a primary subject.
   - Every sentence in a paragraph must be relevant to the primary subject. After the discussion of the primary subject concludes, so does the paragraph.
   - Do not combine two or more primary subjects into a paragraph.

   The two main causes of a faulty paragraph are including irrelevant sentences and adding a second subject. When reviewing paragraphs, simply answer two questions:

   a. Is there only one primary subject?
   b. Is every sentence relevant to the primary subject?

2. *Paragraphs are composed of three formal parts.*
   Paragraphs consist of:

   a. a topic sentence,
   b. supporting sentence(s), and
   c. a concluding sentence.

3. *The topic sentence is the first sentence of a paragraph.*
   The purpose of the topic sentence is to introduce the primary subject of the paragraph. It should be the most general sentence in the paragraph, meaning that it will have the fewest details of any other sentence in the paragraph.

4. *Supporting sentences are in the group from the second sentence to the second-last sentence.*
   The purpose of the supporting sentences is to explain the topic sentence or have relevance to it. Although there is no universal minimum number of supporting sentences, five to seven has been accepted by some as the minimum needed. Police reports are dependent on circumstances and elicited information, which vary substantially. Consequently, a minimum number should not always be the primary objective. Instead, the goal of supporting sentences in a GOR narrative should be to include only those that are relevant to the topic sentence.

5. *The concluding sentence is the last sentence of a paragraph.*
   The concluding sentence may summarize the primary subject or it may simply be the last relevant circumstance that explains the primary subject. It should signify that the discussion of that subject has ended.

6. *Paragraphs must be sequentially ordered.*
   All narratives have multiple subjects or topics. Each one must be accurately identified and placed in logical sequence. The sequential order of paragraphs creates a seamless path of information. A narrative produces *outcomes*, referring to types of information learned by the reader. Two types of outcomes emerge from narratives:

   a. a general outcome, referring to the totality of the circumstances, or entire story, that the writer intends for the reader to learn; or
   b. specific outcomes, referring to subjects or topics that compose the totality of the circumstances.

5. Apply the RSP System

Refer back to Chapter 5, page 23, for a diagram of the RSP system, which can be applied when writing any GOR narrative.

There are several key points to remember when writing a narrative.

▸ There are four parts of a GOR narrative:

   a. introduction,
   b. before the occurrence,
   c. during the occurrence, and
   d. after the occurrence.

- Each part has a *template* that guides how to write it. Each template incorporates the RSP system.
- Maximum information; minimum words. Convey as much information as possible without the clutter of meaningless words or phrases.
- Do not ignore simplicity. Use simple language that is direct and to the point. Do not try to impress the reader with complicated language, but do meet the expectation of using post-secondary vocabulary. Strike the balance. Do not reduce a narrative to an inferior, substandard short report, but also do not needlessly increase the word count with empty language.
- The most important RSP rule is "turn the abstract into concrete." Replace abstract language with concrete language. This rule ensures achieving the goal of 100 percent accurate understanding by narrowing a broad possible interpretation to a single interpretation.

The following chart includes examples of how to narrow a reader's interpretation by replacing abstract language with concrete.

Abstract	Concrete
‣ vehicle	‣ type of vehicle (e.g., passenger car) with precise description (e.g., white 2004 four-door Ford Taurus)
‣ weapon	‣ type and precise description (e.g., 7 inch kitchen knife)
‣ contacted	‣ specific means of communication with time/date (e.g., phone on Sat. May 5, 2007, at 2:43 p.m.)
‣ proceeded (e.g., "proceeded to the victim's house")	‣ specific means with time/date (e.g., drove to the victim's house on a Harley Davidson motorcycle on Sun. May 6, 2007 at 1:17 a.m.)
‣ indicated (e.g., "he indicated he had been drinking")	‣ verbatim response/quotation (e.g., "the suspect answered, 'I only drank three beers during the past four hours'")
‣ observed (e.g., "I observed the suspect with a weapon")	‣ explain how the observation occurred; use the word "saw" with precise conduct (e.g., "I saw the suspect holding a 7 inch kitchen knife in his right hand")
‣ detected (e.g., "I detected alcohol consumption")	‣ explain how the detection was made (e.g., "I smelled an alcoholic beverage on the suspect's breath")
‣ discovered (e.g., "a weapon was discovered in the vehicle")	‣ explain how and where the discovery was made, and what exactly was found ‣ use words such as *searched* and *seized*, accompanied by precise descriptions of places and items

The following is a list of common abstract words and phrases that must be avoided and replaced with concrete language.

a number of times in the past

abusive

adverse

aggressive

agitated

approached

assaulted

attempted

breached

careless

communicated

criminal record

damaged

dangerous

defrauded

denied

disturbance

escaped

fabricated

failed to comply

forced

forcibly

fraudulently

harassed

has displayed inappropriate behaviour

has disregarded warnings

hostile

impaired

imported

incriminated

injured/injuries

insulting

loitered

menacingly

negligent

obscene

obstructed

occasionally

offensive

often

participated

possessed

profane

refused

resisted

robbed

struggled

threatened

trafficked

trespassed

uncooperative

unsafe

used

uttered

violently

vulgar

witnessed

WRITING THE "INTRODUCTION"

An *introduction* is the first of four parts of a GOR narrative.

The narrative is composed of two parts:

1. response
2. arrival.

The following are samples of the two parts:

Response	At 21:26 hrs, police responded to 3001 Thunder Road regarding a belated break, enter, and theft.	OR	At 21:26 hrs, Doug Heaton attended at 51 Division (police station) to report a belated break, enter, and theft that occurred at his house at 3001 Thunder Road. He reported the following:
Arrival	Upon arrival at 21:29 hrs, writer was met by Doug Heaton who reported the following: Heaton is 50 years old. He is legally married to his wife, Claire Heaton (50). They own a dwelling-house situated at 3001 Thunder Road. They are self-employed and own XYZ Chemical Company Inc. They have two sons, Justin (21) and Andrew (19). Both are students at Smith College. Both live at home. The suspect is Jake Mezzomatto, 19 years old, 5045 Colts Drive. He is Andrew's friend.		

The examples above refer to a *belated–reactive* investigation. This is the most common front-line police investigation, and the simplest of the four types. It is the starting point for learning the remaining types of narrative, and serves as a point of reference to help you progress to other reports.

The goal of a belated–reactive introduction is to inform the reader about:

- the source of the call (how you received the call);
- your observations upon arrival;
- the participants (complainant, witnesses, suspects);
- the place (crime scene); and
- times/dates.

The introduction allows the reader to form a vivid mental image about:

- *how* you received the call (referred to as the *response method*);
- *when* you arrived;
- *what* you saw, and did upon arrival;
- *where* the crime scene is and its appearance; and
- *who* is involved (victims, witnesses, suspects).

Response

There are only two general "response" methods for a belated–reactive call:

1. radio broadcast (you go to the victim at the crime scene); or
2. police station (the victim/witness attends at the police station).

Arrival

The "arrival" part of the introduction includes:

- the time of arrival;
- the first person met (the starting point of information gathering); and
- the participants and place.

1. *Time of arrival*: Example: Upon arrival at 21:29 hrs …
2. *First person met*: The "first person met" is the reader's starting point on a pathway of information.
3. *Participants and place*: Participants and place familiarize the reader with fundamental information before events are explained. The important elements are:
   - participants
     a. age, address, occupation, employment
     b. marital status
     c. other occupants at primary participant's address
     d. what property/items are owned
     e. information relevant to the occurrence
   - place
     a. design (how the place is constructed). Examples include:
       - type: dwelling (house or commercial)
       - style: number of floors, rooms, size
       - entrances: number and location (i.e., visibility to other people)
       - structures: garage, shed, fences, yards, property
       - contextual location: suburb, urban, mall, industrial complex
     b. appearance. Examples include:
       - existence of property/items (e.g., furniture, bodily substances, weapons)
       - position of these items

Introduction Template
(Belated–Reactive Occurrence)

Response	At (time/date), (police or officer's name) responded to (place—business name/address) regarding (the precise radio broadcast call—e.g., 911, unknown problem, domestic)
	OR
	At (time/date), (name of person) attended at (name of police station) to report a (nature of occurrence) at (place).
	Mr./Mrs./Ms. (surname) reported the following:
	_____
	_____
	_____
Arrival	Upon arrival at (time), writer was met by (name of first person met), who reported the following:
	He/she is (age). He/she lives at/owns (place). He/she is (marital status—partner name/age). They have (children: name(s) and age(s)) or no children. Mr./Mrs. (name) is a (occupation) and works at (place). Mr./Mrs. (partner name) is a (occupation) and works at (place). (Name of place/house) is a (style, size, rooms, entrances). There is/are (structures—garage, fence, yard). It is situated in (contextual location—mall, urban area, suburb, industrial area).

WRITING THE EVENTS
"BEFORE THE OCCURRENCE"

This is the *pre-offence* stage that represents the second part of the narrative. The time period varies. The pre-offence stage starts whenever the first relevant act occurs and ends immediately before the *actus reus*.

The *first relevant act* is defined as the starting point that proves either:

▸ victim credibility, or
▸ any fact-in-issue (who committed the crime and why).

The focus of the pre-offence stage is:

▸ the suspect's intent and opportunity (e.g., victim–offender familiarity, suspect's planning, suspect's statements, motive); and
▸ witness credibility (e.g., physical condition, mental condition, position relating to observation).

Follow the steps below when completing the pre-offence section of a GOR narrative.

1. Describe the complainant's activity preceding the offence—generally, what the complainant did on the offence date, and specifically:
   ▸ the presence or absence of alcohol or drug consumption;
   ▸ conversation with potential suspects;
   ▸ awareness/attention immediately before the offence;
   ▸ locking premises or securing money or property; and
   ▸ all other relevant acts pertaining to identifying suspects and the commission of the offence.
2. Identify all witnesses so they may be contacted later. Describe their activity preceding the offence.
3. Outline the complainant's past history, specifically explaining interactions with potential suspects.
4. Record verbal or written statements made by potential suspects to the complainant and other witnesses.
5. Note any relevant circumstance that proves any degree of motive or intent by a person to commit the offence.
6. Explain all circumstances that demonstrate planning by an offender.
7. Use the 10-point list of witness credibility factors as a guideline.

The following is a summation from the supplementary textbook, *Criminal Investigation*. Refer to this text for complete details on the use of this investigative strategy.

The 10-Point List

The "10-point list" is a procedural guideline that can be used to justify an opinion about credibility. It is an informal procedure only; it is not a law. The list includes 10 factors that should be considered when evaluating credibility. The factors are derived from a combination of case law decisions and personal experience.

The first objective of this list is to determine the presence or absence of each factor. Afterward, the 10-point list is applied to the information reported to determine compatibility, which helps justify an opinion of strong or weak credibility.

1. *Acquisition position*: Determine whether the witness was actually present during the offence and, if so, whether the witness's position allowed acquisition of the observation.
2. *Intent to learn*: This refers to prior attention focused on the crime area and to an awareness that a crime was about to occur. Determine where the witness's attention was before the offence happened and the reasons why.

   For example, a pedestrian may be standing on a sidewalk at an intersection waiting to cross. Two cars collide in the intersection. Commonly, the sound of the collision causes the witness to look. The witness sees the aftermath, if the noise created the attention. In this case, nothing happened before the collision that drew his or her attention to either car. Consequently, no intent to learn existed. No awareness of the incident means that the witness likely did not see the event happen but saw only the result. In the same case, awareness of one of the cars may have been caused by squealing tires, excessive speed, or some other unusual act. The attention to the cars created the intent to learn the event by raising an awareness that some incident may be about to occur. The existence of the intent to learn suggests that the witness likely saw the entire incident occur and should be able to recall and report a substantial number of details about the event. Focused attention ensures optimum acquisition of the observation.

The existence or absence of the intent to learn is compatible with the amount of information reported.

- The existence of the intent to learn and a lengthy, detailed statement are compatible, indicating strong credibility.
- The absence of the intent to learn and few or no details are compatible, indicating strong credibility. It is logical that nothing was seen if no prior awareness existed.
- The existence of the intent to learn and a brief statement are not compatible, indicating weak credibility. The witness may be withholding information. If prior awareness existed, the witness logically should have observed more than is being reported.
- The absence of the intent to learn and a lengthy, detailed statement are not compatible, indicating weak credibility. If no prior awareness existed, the witness likely would not have seen the entire incident. It is logical to suspect that some details may be intentionally fabricated or simply assumed as opposed to actual observations.

3. *Duration of observation*: The length of time a witness observed a person or an occurrence may substantially increase the witness's accuracy.[1] There is no specific time that constitutes sufficient duration of observation. It is difficult to accurately determine whether a witness had enough time to acquire an observation, particularly the facial features of an offender. One method that helps is asking if the witness had any conversation with the offender. Dialogue tends to focus attention facially. If a conversation did occur, you have a strong indication that sufficient duration existed. Otherwise, there needs to be some element that drew attention, such as an offender's possession of a weapon, which will suggest the witness had enough time to make optimum acquisition.

4. *Retention period*: This refers to the interval between the time of observation (offence) and time of recall (interview). The time that elapses may affect the accuracy of recall. Which is better for accuracy, a short or long retention period? It depends on a process called *rehearsal*. If an observation is repeated continually, it transfers from short-term memory to long-term memory. If no rehearsal or repetition occurs, the observation stays in short-term memory. Observations in short-term memory are lost quickly, usually in less than 30 seconds.[2] If repetition occurs, the observation may transfer to long-term memory, becoming a permanent memory that lasts a lifetime.[3] Therefore, a longer retention period may afford the witness the time to rehearse or repeat the

observation and transfer it to long-term memory. The problems with longer retention, however, outweigh the advantages.

- ▸ Short-term memory is easily disrupted. An interruption or distraction may result in the loss of information within a few seconds.[4]
- ▸ There is no specific number of repetitions or specific time of rehearsal that will always result in a transfer to long-term memory. It is a vague concept that cannot be measured or determined accurately. The interviewing officer will not be able to positively determine that the witness has transferred the observation to long-term memory.
- ▸ Ebbinghaus's Forgetting Curve measures retention at various time intervals. This experiment shows that forgetting begins very quickly after acquiring information and then gradually tapers off. A significant amount of forgetting can occur within the first 24 hours of acquiring information. (See Chapter 6, page 56, for more detail regarding this study.)

In summary, a longer time between the offence and the interview will likely result in substantial forgetting. A short interval will enhance recall and prevent a significant loss of information.

5. *Interference with mental repetition during the retention period*: Repeating information mentally is essential for transferring observations from short-term to long-term memory. After a witness sees an offence, distractions and interruptions will likely occur, causing a loss of information within seconds. Witnesses acquire other information after the offence from other people, or by seeing something, or by having to think of other things, such as dialing a telephone. These events disrupt short-term memory. In other words, the less a witness has to think about or is distracted by after the offence and before the interview, the more information that may be accurately recalled. Witnesses should be asked about what they did during the time between the offence and interview to determine if mental repetition was disrupted.

6. *Sensory problems*: These refer to vision or hearing problems and also include inaccurate perception of details such as height, weight, age, and distances.

7. *Alcohol or drug consumption*: See the supplementary textbook, *Criminal Investigation*, for a discussion of the effects of these two substances.

8. *Excessive stress*: Stress can be informally divided into three categories. Excessive or high stress levels may affect observation by narrowing focus on a weapon, for example. See the supplementary textbook, *Criminal Investigation*, for a full discussion.

9. *Conformity*: Discussion among witnesses after an offence may cause a witness to adopt incorrect observations, simply to conform with the observations of others.

10. *Motive to lie*: The common reasons for witness deception were explained in previous chapters.

Example

The complainant, Creighton, has known the suspect, Tom Joad, for 12 years. They have been occasional workout partners and have socialized together frequently. In June 2006, they were drinking at Ike's Bar, situated at 5527 Western Rd. Creighton asked to burrow $500 from Joad. After some discussion, Joad agreed to lend Creighton $500 and conditions of payment were made. Creighton agreed to pay Joad $550 on January 1, 2007 to cover the coast of the loan and subsequent interest.

On January 5, 2007, at 20:15 hrs, Creighton and Joad met a Pasquale's Bar, situated at 5045 Haltom Rd. Joad asked Creighton for the $550. Creighton apologized and asked for an extension to re-pay the money. Joad agreed to extend the payment date to January 31, 2007. The conversation was amiable.

No other conversation occurred between them until January 31, 2007, at 21:00 hrs. At the time, Creighton was sitting in the living room of his house. The phone rang. He answered it. The following conversation occurred:

Caller:	"Do you have my money?"
Creighton:	"Sorry, I can't pay you back."
Caller:	"You can't pay me back?" (Shouting)
Creighton:	"No, I lost all the money gambling."
Caller:	"You punk." (Shouting)

The caller hung up at that time. The caller's voice, in Creighton's opinion, was Joad. During the past 12 years, they have had numerous phone conversations.

Gloria Doors was visiting Joad, at his house, at the time of the call. Joad had been her boyfriend for 18 months. On January 31, 2007, at about 20:55 hrs, Doors and Joad were sitting on a coach in the living rooms of Joan's house. Joad said to Doors, "I'm calling Creighton. He owes me money today." Doors saw Joad pick up a phone that was on a table next to the couch. After dialing the number, Doors heard Joad say the following: "Do you have my money?" (pause), "You can't pay me back?" (pause), and then shouted, "You punk." Joad slammed the phone down and screamed, "That loser. I'm going to kill him." Doors saw Joad walk out the front door. One minute later, she heard a car starting in the driveway. She looked through the living room window. She saw Joad's car travelling eastbound on Brantford Ave.

After the second phase of the narrative is complete, the reader will have a vivid mental image of the events leading up to the moment when the offence began.

WRITING THE EVENTS "DURING THE OCCURRENCE"

The third phase of the narrative must precisely describe the *actus reus*, or physical act, of the offence. Generally, there are two types of *actus reus* narratives. The first is an explanation based on eyewitness observations. The second is explained by circumstantial evidence, referring to a series of events or situations that lead to a logical conclusion or opinion, in the absence of direct evidence such as eyewitness observation. The eyewitness-based narrative generally has more information than the circumstantial-oriented narrative.

Follow the steps below when completing this section of a GOR narrative.

1. Refer to the statute and section that identify the offence being reported. Describe the facts-in-issue that compose the *actus reus*. This represents the target or focus of this part of the narrative.

2. The information in this part must be relevant to the facts-in-issue of the *actus reus*. Avoid either irrelevant information or that which did not occur during the offence.

3. Describe the position of the complainant and witnesses at the beginning of and throughout their observations.

4. Explain the presence or absence of factors that may affect witness observation.

5. Do not describe an act with the name of an offence (e.g., assault, threaten). Instead, describe the act by explaining the precise words or conduct that constituted the offence. See the following examples.

   ‣ Instead of "threaten," state the words verbatim.
   ‣ Instead of "assault," explain the object that caused the force and the specific nature of the force (e.g., Virgil punched Ike with his right fist, striking his jaw).
   ‣ Instead of "rob," describe the theft and the violence (e.g., Ike held a butcher knife in his right hand, raised it to shoulder-level height, pointed the blade about one metre from her face and said, "Give me all the money or I'll kill you.")

6. Use concrete explanations. Do not use abstract phrases exclusively. Among the many common abstract phrases used in narrative is the word "forced."

   ‣ "The door was *forced* open."
   ‣ "He *forced* his way into the house" or "He entered by *forcible* means."

   These abstract explanations are open to a wide range of interpretations. In each example, replace the abstract phrase.

   ‣ "The door was open. The frame and the door were both damaged. The wood was splintered near the door handle."
   ‣ "Virgil stood in the doorway and told Ike to leave. Virgil tried to close the door. Ike pushed the door with his shoulder and walked in."

   These concrete explanations allow the reader to conclude undoubtedly that force was used, without using the word "force" or "forcible." There is only one interpretation in these explanations.

   It is acceptable to precede a concrete explanation with an abstract introduction. For example, "Ike forced his way in by (explain with concrete words)"; "The door was forced opened by (explain with concrete words)."

7. Do not paraphrase an offender's verbal statements. What an offender says during an offence is relevant to prove *mens rea*. Write the quote verbatim.

8. If multiple witnesses exist, record each individual's observation separately. When more than one witness sees an offence, it is unlikely they will report precisely the same observations. Separate reports will allow the detective an opportunity to evaluate the credibility of each witness. Combining all witness observations into one general narrative will interfere with case management.

9. Describe persons and items systematically. Persons and items are described by two categories of characteristics:

    a. general, and

    b. specific (see page 48 for definitions of these characteristics).

    General characteristics are described first, followed by specific characteristics.

10. State whether or not each witness can facially recognize the offender.

Example (eyewitness-based narrative)

On January 31, 2007, at 21:15 hrs, Creighton was sitting in the living room of his house. The front door was unlocked. The living room window was situated 3 metres from his couch. He had a clear view of the street in front of his house. Creighton was home alone.

He saw a white BMW stop along the curb, directly in front of his house. He saw Tom Joad exit the car via the driver's door. Creighton has known Joad for three years. Joad was wearing a white t-shirt with a red "X" on the front, and blue jeans. The distance between Creighton and Joad was 10 metres. The view was unobstructed. Joad walked toward the front entrance. Creighton remained on the couch.

The front door opened. No announcement was made. Joad walked in, yelled, "You punk," walked to Creighton, and punched Creighton six times in the face with his right fist. Joad walked to the front door and left the house. Creighton walked to the bathroom. He took a towel and wiped blood from his nose. He walked to the living room and phoned the police.

WRITING THE EVENTS "AFTER THE OFFENCE"

The final stage of the narrative is the *post-offence* stage that includes:

- ▸ the suspect's post-offence conduct; and
- ▸ police post-offence investigation strategy and acts.

This part explains the relevant events that occurred between the time that the *actus reus* ended and the time that the first officer's preliminary investigation concluded.

Follow the steps below when completing the post-offence section of a GOR narrative. Record:

1. statements made by an offender to anyone (citizen or police);
2. discovery, seizure, transfer, concealing, or destruction of physical evidence;
3. the offender's means of departure and potential destination;
4. the offender's possessions, and analysis of the crime scene;
5. alteration to the crime scene; and
6. circumstances that form mere suspicion or reasonable grounds.

Example (events after the crime)

Joad walked to his car, entered it and drove to his house. He arrived there at 21:38 hrs. He walked into the house through the front door. Doors was sitting on the living room couch. Joad was holding his right hand with his left hand. He said to her, "Get me some ice." Doors asked, "What happened?" Joad responded, "I punched out Creighton." Doors walked into the kitchen, placed ice on a towel, returned to the living room, and wrapped the ice and towel on Joan's right hand. Doors saw bloodstains on the front of Joad's white t-shirt.

At 21:26 hrs, Cst. Hec arrived at Creighton's house. The front door was open one metre. There was no damage to the door. Creighton was interviewed inside the house. Creighton's nose was bleeding. He declined medical attention. Creighton dictated a written statement to Cst. Hec. At the conclusion of the statement, Creighton read it and signed it.

At 22:00 hrs, Cst. Hec arrived at Joad's house and knocked on the front door. Doors answered the door and invited Cst. Hec to enter. Doors was interviewed. She informed police that Joad left five minutes earlier, on foot. He did not inform her about his destination. She gave Cst. Hec a formal, written witness statement.

Investigation continues.

GOR SAMPLES—BELATED-REACTIVE OCCURRENCES

The following information is specific to each GOR found on pages 80–100, and is meant to summarize the OR component of the occurrence. Each sample is of an occurrence where no arrest was made during the preliminary investigation.

1. *Radio broadcast: Belated theft from auto* (Sample 1—pages 80–83)
   Offence recognition: a motor vehicle is not a "place" in relation to break and enter offences. Consequently, the offence is theft under $5,000. Break and enter offences do not apply to forcible entry into cars.

2. *Radio broadcast: Belated theft* (Sample 2—pages 84–86)
   Offence recognition: Money was stolen from a wallet inside an unlocked locker situated in an unlocked high school dressing room. The suspect entered two "places"—an unlocked dressing room and a locker. A "place" for break and enter purposes involves a "structure." Case law defines a structure as a place inside which human beings can function. The dressing room is a structure; the locker is not. According to the definitions of "break and enter." The suspect committed the offence of break, enter, and theft if there was no consent to enter and if the suspect entered with the intent to commit an **indictable offence**. Given the implied consent to enter an unlocked high school change room, combined with the possibility that *mens rea* was formed after legitimate entry occurred, the report was classified as "theft under $5,000."

3. *Radio broadcast: Disturbance* (Sample 3—pages 87–88)
   Offence recognition: Cause a disturbance is a **summary conviction offence**. The police must find committing to arrest but may change within six months based on a reasonable grounds belief. The offence must occur in a public place, not a dwelling-house. Evidence is needed to prove specific

abstract behaviour such as fighting, shouting, and using obscene language. In this case, obscene language was used. The actual words are required in notebooks, reports, and testimony. For this example, the entire obscenity will not be printed; only the first letter will be used. Finally, if the offenders have departed prior to police arrival, a report is required to document the criminal offences that occurred. The offenders' departure does not negate the fact that the offence occurred.

4. *Radio broadcast: Disturbance* (Sample 4—pages 89–91)
   Offence recognition: This type of radio broadcast suggests that an offence is "in progress." In some cases an assault occurs. The person who calls the police often generalizes and reports that a "fight" or "disturbance" is occurring. In this case, one person assaulted another. The extent of the injury did not constitute "bodily harm." The report was entitled "assault."

5. *Radio broadcast: Belated break and enter* (Sample 5—pages 92–94)
   Offence recognition: This example intends to show how to write a break and enter report that occurred at a house, in the past.

6. *Radio broadcast: Alarm* (Sample 6—pages 95–97)
   Offence recognition: An alarm signifies the potential of an "in-progress" offence. In this case, a break and enter occurred at a building other than a dwelling-house. A theft occurred inside. This report shows the difference between a belated and an in-progress break and enter.

7. *Radio broadcast: Missing person* (Sample 7—pages 98–100)
   Offence recognition: This report explains the preliminary investigation pertaining to the absence of a 14-year-old. The focus of the investigation is finding the missing person and determining whether a criminal offence occurred. If no evidence proves the commission of an offence, the report is entitled "missing person" until a conclusion is reached.

Sample 1: Belated Theft from Auto

General Incident ☑ Arrest Report ☐

Request for Summons ☐ 3

YOUNG OFFENDER ☐

NO. OF SUPPLEMENTARY REPORTS

DESCRIPTION OF PROPERTIES OR INJURIES (INC. SERIAL NOS.) VALUE DAMAGED RECOVERED
INJURIES: MAJOR ☐ MINOR ☐ NONE ☐

See narrative

SPECIFY ON SUPPLEMENTARY: TYPE OF INJURIES SUSTAINED. TYPE OF FORCED USED. SUFFICIENT DETAILS FOR PLEA OF GUILTY. CO-ACCUSED, PREVIOUS ADDRESS OF ACCUSED, ETC.

FOR NARRATIVE COMPLETE SUPPLEMENTARY REPORT

DATE & TIME OF ARREST   ARRESTING OFFICER
LOCATION OF ARREST   HAZARD ☐
CHARGES (IF WARRANT EXECUTED, STATE TYPE)

NOTIFICATIONS: Y.O.A. – NOTICE TO PARENT SERVED ☐ YES ☐ NO
OTHERS: ☐ SPOUSE ☐ GUARDIAN ☐ OTHER – NAME:
         ☐ PARENT ☐ NEXT OF KIN
ADDRESS   HOME PHONE
ARRESTED FOR OTHER DEPT. (NAME)   WHO NOTIFIED?   TIME   YR. MO. DAY
RELEASED TO (NAME/RANK/No.)   TIME

BAIL HEARING YES ☐ NO ☐
FINGERPRINT DATE   FORM OF RELEASE
BAIL & RELEASE RECOMMENDATIONS   STATEMENT TAKEN YES ☐ NO ☐
CNI/CPIC QUERIED? RESULTS
RELEASED BY OFFICER   NAME J.P.
DATE & TIME OF RELEASE   COURT   COURT DATE & TIME
HAZARD REMARKS (MUST BE COMPLETED IF HAZARD CHECKED)

STATS. CANADA CLEARED BY   ADULTS JUVENILES INF.
CHARGE OTHER UNF.   INCIDENT CLASS   M F   M F

OFFICE ONLY DATA ENTRY DATA VERIF.   DATA RECEIVED IN RECORDS   DATE CLEARED

DIVISION 33   PATROL AREA/ZONE 51-51   INCIDENT CLASS   INCIDENT NO. 07-3001

TYPE OF INCIDENT Theft under $5,000.00   TIME & DATE OF INCIDENT (TIME OR BETWEEN) 17:10   YR. 07 MO. MAR DAY 03 HAZARD ☐

LOCATION OF INCIDENT Parking lot behind 56 Garrison Rd., Welland, ON

HOW INCIDENT COMMITTED See narrative   MEANS (WEAPONS, TOOLS USED) See narrative

VICTIM / COMPLAINANT
SURNAME Doors   GIVEN(1) Gloria   GIVEN(2)   RACE WHITE ☑ NON-WHITE ☐
ADDRESS 56 Garrison Rd., Upper Apt., Welland, ON   HOME PHONE 905-555-3001 (EXT./LOCAL)
SEX F YR. 82 DOB MO. 15 DAY 12 MAR. ST. S OCCUPATION Manager   BUSINESS PHONE 905-714-4545
PLACE OF EMPLOYMENT/EMPLOYER X Fitness   HAZARD ☐

REPORTED BY
SURNAME Same   GIVEN(1)   GIVEN(2)   GIVEN(3)
ADDRESS   HOME PHONE   (EXT./LOCAL)
SEX YR. DOB MO. DAY   RELATIONSHIP TO VICTIM/COMPLAINANT   CONDITION Sober ☐ Intox ☐ HBD ☐ Drugs ☐ HAZARD ☐
PLACE OF EMPLOYMENT/EMPLOYER   BUSINESS PHONE

VEH. USED
TYPE   LICENCE No.   LIC. YR. LIC. PROV. VEH. YR. MAKE MODEL
STYLE   COLOUR   VIN
OWNER SAME ☐ SURNAME   GIVEN(1)   ADDRESS
OUTSTANDING FEATURES

ACCUSED / SUSPECT
SURNAME   GIVEN(1)   GIVEN(2)   NICK NAMES   ALIAS ☐ NÉE ☐
ADDRESS   HAZARD ☐ RACE   HOME PHONE   WHITE ☐ NON-WHITE ☐
SEX YR. DOB MO. DAY AGE MAR. ST. MHT(HT) WGT(WT) EYES-COLOUR DESCRIPTION OF CLOTHING
HAIR COLOUR
BUILD ☐ SLENDER ☐ MEDIUM ☐ HEAVY   HAIR TYPE ☐ BALD ☐ PART BALD ☐ SHORT ☐ LONG ☐ STRAIGHT ☐ CURLY/WAVY ☐ WELL DRESSED ☐ UNKEMPT ☐ BUSHY   COMPLEXION ☐ SALLOW ☐ LIGHT/FAIR ☐ RUDDY ☐ FRECKLED ☐ DARK/SWARTHY ☐ POCK-MARKED   ☐ GLASSES ☐ CONTACT LENS   TEETH ☐ GOOD ☐ IRREGULAR ☐ FALSE ☐ VISIBLE GOLD ☐ STAINED ☐ PROTRUD. UPPERS ☐ PROTRUD. LOWERS ☐ VISIBLE DECAY ☐ VISIBLE MISSING
MOUSTACHE ☐ BEARD ☐ WIG ☐
VICTIM/ACCUSED RELATIONSHIP   DRIVER'S LICENCE No.   PROV.   N.R.P. No.
PHYSICAL/MENTAL CONDITION, MARKS, SCARS, TATTOOS, OUTSTANDING FEATURES   F.P.S. No.
CNI CAUTION V ☐ E ☐ A ☐   CONDITION Sober ☐ Intox ☐ HBD ☐ Drugs ☐   OCCUPATION
            M ☐ S ☐ O ☐   GRADE
PLACE OF EMPLOYMENT/EMPLOYER/SCHOOL/GRADE   BUS. PHONE   (EXT./LOCAL)

REPORTING OFFICER (FULL NAME/RANK/NO.) Creighton H. CST #362   DATE/TIME REPORT TAKEN YR. 07 MO. MAR DAY 03 TIME 17:40
OTHER OFFICER(S) ATTENDING   I.D. OFFICER RESPONDING

REPORT CHECKED BY (FULL NAME/RANK/NO.)   CASE REASSIGNED TO   BY   DATE
REPORT CHECKED BY (FULL NAME/RANK/NO.)   INCIDENT STATUS (IF INVEST.COMP.CHECK SOLVED OR UNSOLVED) INVEST. CONT. ☐ INVEST. COMP. ☐ SOLVED ☐ UNSOLVED ☐   INIT./DATE

Sample 1   (Continued)

Supplementary Report

CHECK APPROPRIATE BOX

ORIGINAL INCIDENT ☐
ARREST ☒
VEHICLE ☐

MISSING PERSON/ELOPEE ☒
FRAUDULENT DOCUMENT ☐
HOMICIDE/SUDDEN DEATH ☒
OTHER ☐

SURNAME(OR NAME & TYPE OF BUSINESS)
Doors, Gloria

DIVISION	PATROL AREA/ZONE	INCIDENT CLASS	INCIDENT No.
33	51-51		07-3001

TYPE OF INCIDENT
Theft under $5,000.00

DATE OF ORIGINAL REPORT
07-03-03

REFERENCE

VICTIM/COMPLAINANT ☒

POLICE INFORMATION ☐
ACCUSED ☐
(EXT./LOCAL)

BUS. PHONE (EXT./LOCAL)
905-714-4545

HOME PHONE
905-555-3001

HAZARD ☐

ADDRESS
56 Garrison Rd., Upper Apt., Welland, ON

At 17:40 hrs, police attended at 56 Garrison Road, regarding a belated theft from auto. Upon arrival, the officer was met by Gloria Doors, who reported the following:

She is 20 years old and lives in the upper apartment at 56 Garrison Rd., above X Fitness, a 24-hour gym where she is employed as manager. She owns a 1992 Mazda Presidia, 2-door, black, Ontario registration FR2509.

At 15:00 hrs, she arrived at 56 Garrison Rd. after leaving Niagara College where she had attended journalism classes from 8:30–14:30 hrs. She parked her car in a private lot situated behind X Fitness. There are three parking spaces that adjoin the north wall of X Fitness. This parking lot leads to a private road that is situated in a north–south direction between Garrison Rd. and the back entrance of the Bingo Palace, 51 East Main St. The X Fitness parking lot is situated in the centre of a populated business district. Another large parking lot is situated across from the X Fitness parking lot. There were six cars parked there at 15:00 hrs. There is heavy pedestrian traffic leading to the Bingo Palace entrance, consistently between 12:00–24:00 hrs. An apartment above 54 Garrison Rd. has a door and a window that affords the occupants a clear view of the parking spot occupied by Doors's Mazda.

Doors locked her car at 15:00 hrs. Two items were on the front passenger seat:

1. a Sony digital camera, silver; serial number MX7878; value = $650

2. a Bruce Springsteen CD with "The Rising" printed on the cover; a white sticker with a red "X Fitness" logo printed on it was on the back of the CD plastic case; value = $25

HAZARD REMARKS   (MUST BE COMPLETED IF HAZARD CHECKED)

STATS. CAN CLEARED BY	CHG.	OTHER	UNF.	INCIDENT CLASS	ADULTS M F	JUVENILES M F	INF.
OFFICE ONLY	DATA ENTRY	DATA VERIF.		DATA RECEIVED IN RECORDS		DATE CLEARED	

DATE/TIME OF THIS REPORT

	YR	MO.	DAY	TIME
O	7	M A R	0 3	17:40

I.D. OFFICER REPORTING

REPORTING OFFICER (FULL NAME/RANK/No.)
Creighton H. Cst #362

OTHER OFFICER(S) ATTENDING

CASE REASSIGNED TO

REPORT CHECKED BY (FULL NAME/RANK/No.)   BY   DATE

REPORT CHECKED BY (FULL NAME/RANK/No.)   INIT./DATE

INCIDENT STATUS (IF INVEST. COMP. CHECK SOLVED OR UNSOLVED)
INVEST. CONT. ☐   INVEST. COMP. ☐   SOLVED ☐   UNSOLVED ☐

PAGE No.
1

Sample 1 (Continued)

Supplementary Report

CHECK APPROPRIATE BOX

ORIGINAL	☒
ARREST	☐
INCIDENT	☒
VEHICLE	☐

MISSING PERSON/ELOPEE ☐
FRAUDULENT DOCUMENT ☐
HOMICIDE/SUDDEN DEATH ☐
OTHER ☐

DIVISION 33

PATROL AREA/ZONE 51-51

INCIDENT CLASS

INCIDENT NO. 07-3001

REFERENCE ~~VICTIM~~/COMPLAINANT ☒

POLICE INFORMATION ☐
ACCUSED ☐

TYPE OF INCIDENT Theft under $5,000.00

DATE OF ORIGINAL REPORT 07-03-03

BUS. PHONE (EXT./LOCAL) 905-714-4545

HOME PHONE (EXT./LOCAL) 905-555-3001

HAZARD ☐

SURNAME(OR NAME & TYPE OF BUSINESS) Doors, Gloria

ADDRESS 56 Garrison Rd., Upper Apt., Welland, ON

She entered X Fitness and began working.

At 17:20 hrs, Doors walked to her car, intending to drive to a mall to purchase supplies. She saw the driver's door window shattered; glass fragments were scattered on both front seats. The driver's door was closed and unlocked. The camera and CD were missing from the front seat. The damage was estimated at $150.

While she inspected her car, a man walked out of the upstairs apartment of 54 Garrison Road. He introduced himself as VIRGIL PERDITION (about 35 years) and informed Doors of the following:

He lives in the upstairs apartment at 56 Garrison Rd, with his wife. At 17:10 hrs, he was home alone preparing to leave for work. He was standing at his kitchen sink. A window is situated above it, on the north side of the building, affording a clear view of the X Fitness parking lot. He saw a man riding a bicycle behind his apartment. Mr. Perdition became suspicious because the cyclist stopped, looked at the Mazda briefly, and then parked the bicycle, leaning it against the wall. Mr. Perdition's suspicion increased because he knew that the bingo traffic had stopped, because a session had started at 17:00 hrs, and there would be no potential witnesses at 17:10 hrs.

Mr. Perdition saw the cyclist walk toward the Mazda and pick up a 2x4 piece of wood that was in a pile behind X Fitness. The suspect tried to open the driver's door and then struck the window with the piece of wood. The suspect reached inside, opened the driver's door, and entered the car briefly. He could not see what the suspect took. The suspect ran to his bike and put something in his jacket pockets. He saw the suspect ride the bike eastbound toward the back of the Post Office and lost sight of him.

PAGE NO. 2

DATE/TIME OF THIS REPORT							**TIME** 17:40
	O	YR 7	M	A	R	0 3	

I.D. OFFICER REPORTING

REPORTING OFFICER (FULL NAME/RANK/NO.) Creighton H. CST #362

OTHER OFFICER(S) ATTENDING

REPORT CHECKED BY (FULL NAME/RANK/NO.)

REPORT CHECKED BY (FULL NAME/RANK/NO.)

CASE REASSIGNED TO

INCIDENT STATUS (IF INVEST. COMP. CHECK SOLVED OR UNSOLVED)
INVEST. CONT. ☐ INVEST.COMP. ☐ SOLVED ☐ UNSOLVED ☐

BY

DATE

INIT./DATE

HAZARD REMARKS (MUST BE COMPLETED IF HAZARD CHECKED)

STATS. CAN CLEARED BY	CHG.	OTHER	UNF.	INCIDENT CLASS	ADULTS M F	JUVENILES M F	INF.
OFFICE ONLY	DATA ENTRY	DATA VERIF.		DATA RECEIVED IN RECORDS	DATE CLEARED		

Sample 1 (Concluded)

Supplementary Report

CHECK APPROPRIATE BOX

ORIGINAL	☐	MISSING PERSON/ELOPE	☐
ARREST	☒	FRAUDULENT DOCUMENT	☐
INCIDENT	☒	HOMICIDE/SUDDEN DEATH	☐
VEHICLE	☐	OTHER	☐

SURNAME(OR NAME & TYPE OF BUSINESS)
Doors, Gloria

DIVISION	PATROL AREA/ZONE	INCIDENT CLASS		INCIDENT No.
33	51-51			07-3001

		REFERENCE	POLICE INFORMATION ☐
TYPE OF INCIDENT		~~VICTIM~~ COMPLAINANT ☒	ACCUSED ☐
Theft under $5,000.00			(EXT./LOCAL)

DATE OF ORIGINAL REPORT	BUS. PHONE (EXT./LOCAL)	HOME PHONE
07-03-03	905-714-4545	905-555-3001

HAZARD ☐

ADDRESS
56 Garrison Rd., Upper Apt., Welland, ON

Mr. Perdition described the suspect as follows: male, white, about 25 years, shoulder length curly dark hair (unkempt), clean shaven, no glasses, no hat, waist length navy blue jacket, blue jeans (no description of the bike).

Mr. Perdition has seen this person before, twice during the past week walking behind the apartment, and three or four times during the past month riding a bicycle on East Main St. Mr. Perdition saw the suspect's face while the suspect committed the offence and can recognize him in the future.

He gave Doors no explanation for not calling the police after he saw the offence being committed. Doors phoned the police; Perdition had to leave to attend work. He was gone prior to police arrival. He works at Stelco in Welland.

Writer arrived at 17:40 hrs. The Mazda had not been moved. The shattered glass was still inside the car. The 2x4 piece of wood was on the pavement beneath the driver's door. It was seized for forensic analysis.

Forensic unit was notified to analyze the car.

A search was conducted of bars and streets in the area, with negative results achieved.

Investigation continues

		PAGE No.
		3

DATE/TIME OF THIS REPORT	YR	MO.	DAY	TIME
	07	MAR	03	17:40

I.D. OFFICER REPORTING

REPORTING OFFICER (FULL NAME/RANK/No.)
Creighton H. CST #362

OTHER OFFICER(S) ATTENDING

REPORT CHECKED BY (FULL NAME/RANK/No.)	CASE REASSIGNED TO	BY	DATE

REPORT CHECKED BY (FULL NAME/RANK/No.)	INCIDENT STATUS (IF INVEST. COMP., CHECK SOLVED OR UNSOLVED)		INIT./DATE
	INVEST. CONT. ☐ INVEST.COMP. ☐ SOLVED ☐ UNSOLVED ☐		

HAZARD REMARKS   (MUST BE COMPLETED IF HAZARD CHECKED)

STATS. CAN CLEARED BY	CHG.	OTHER	UNF.	INCIDENT CLASS	ADULTS		JUVENILES		INF.
					M	F	M	F	

OFFICE ONLY	DATA ENTRY	DATA VERIF.	DATA RECEIVED IN RECORDS	DATE CLEARED

Sample 2: Belated Theft

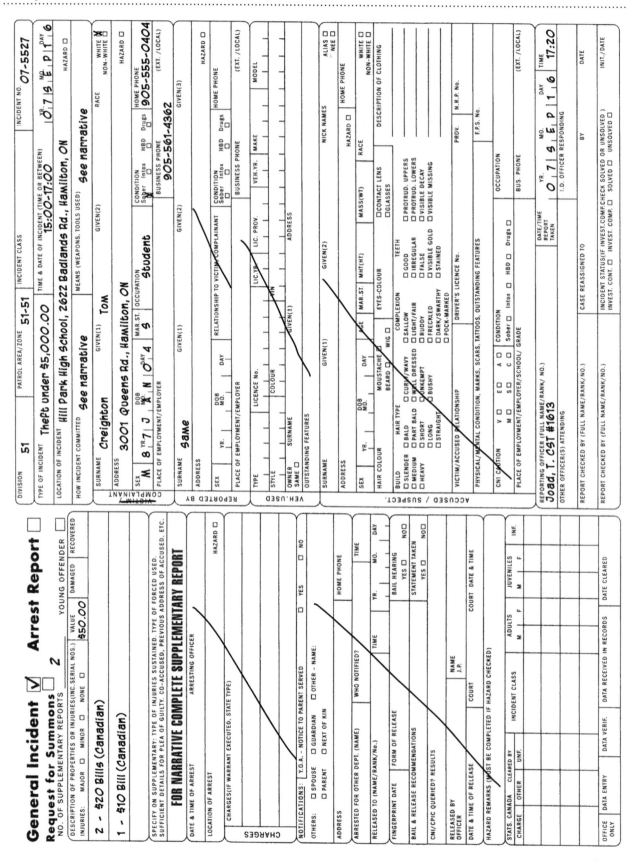

Sample 2   (Continued)

Supplementary Report

CHECK APPROPRIATE BOX

ORIGINAL	☑	MISSING PERSON/ELOPEE	☐
ARREST	☐	FRAUDULENT DOCUMENT	☐
INCIDENT	☑	HOMICIDE/SUDDEN DEATH	☐
VEHICLE	☐	OTHER	☐

DIVISION	PATROL AREA/ZONE	INCIDENT CLASS	INCIDENT No.
51	51-51		07-5527

TYPE OF INCIDENT: Theft under $5,000.00

REFERENCE

	POLICE INFORMATION	☐
VICTIM/COMPLAINANT	☑	ACCUSED	☐
	(EXT./LOCAL)	
		HAZARD	☐

DATE OF ORIGINAL REPORT: 07-09-16

BUS. PHONE (EXT./LOCAL): 905-561-4362

HOME PHONE: 905-555-0404

SURNAME (OR NAME & TYPE OF BUSINESS): Creighton, Tom

ADDRESS: 3001 Queens Rd., Hamilton, ON

At 17:20 hrs, police attended at Hill Park High School, 2622 Badlands Rd., Hamilton, regarding a belated theft. Upon arrival, the officer was met by Tom Creighton, the complainant in this matter. He reported the following:

Creighton is a 16-year-old grade 11 student at Hill Park H.S. where he is a member of the senior football team. The roster consists of 34 students. Practice begins daily at 15:00 hrs and concludes at 17:00 hrs. The football locker room is situated at the west end of the school. It has two entrances. A metal fire door leads to the west parking lot. Entrance cannot be gained from the outside without a key. The second entrance leads to the basketball gym. That door is unlocked during school hours and throughout football practice.

On 07-09-16 at 08:30 hrs, Creighton was at his house. He put $50 in his wallet — two $20 bills and one $10 bill (Canadian currency). He brought the wallet and money to school. The wallet included his birth certificate and SIN card.

At 14:45 hrs, he entered the football locker room. There are 65 metal lockers in the room. Creighton placed the wallet on the top shelf of locker #4. He was the first student to leave the room, at 14:50 hrs. Thirty-three other students were in the room when he left. All were on the football field at 15:00 hrs. Creighton left the locker door unlocked.

Between 15:00–17:00 hrs, 22 basketball players and two coaches were in the gym. It is not known if other people entered the gym during that time.

HAZARD REMARKS   (MUST BE COMPLETED IF HAZARD CHECKED)

STATS. CAN CLEARED BY	CHG.	OTHER	UNF.	INCIDENT CLASS			ADULTS		JUVENILES		INF.
							M	F	M	F	

OFFICE ONLY	DATA ENTRY	DATA VERIF.	DATA RECEIVED IN RECORDS		DATE CLEARED

REPORTING OFFICER (FULL NAME/RANK/No.): Joad, T. CST #1613

OTHER OFFICER(S) ATTENDING:

REPORT CHECKED BY (FULL NAME/RANK/No.):

REPORT CHECKED BY (FULL NAME/RANK/No.):

DATE/TIME OF THIS REPORT: YR 0 3 MO. 9 DEP DAY 1 6 TIME 17:20

I.D. OFFICER REPORTING

CASE REASSIGNED TO: | BY | DATE

INCIDENT STATUS (IF INVEST. COMP., CHECK SOLVED OR UNSOLVED) | INIT./DATE

INVEST. STATUS (IF INVEST. COMP. CHECK SOLVED OR UNSOLVED)
INVEST. CONT. ☐   INVEST. COMP. ☐   SOLVED ☐   UNSOLVED ☐

PAGE No. 1

Sample 2 (Concluded)

Supplementary Report

INCIDENT No. 07-5527

DIVISION 51

PATROL AREA/ZONE 51-51

INCIDENT CLASS

REFERENCE ~~VICTIM~~ COMPLAINANT ☒

POLICE INFORMATION ☐
ACCUSED ☐

CHECK APPROPRIATE BOX

ORIGINAL	☒	MISSING PERSON/ELOPEE	☐
ARREST	☐	FRAUDULENT DOCUMENT	☐
INCIDENT	☒	HOMICIDE/SUDDEN DEATH	☐
VEHICLE	☐	OTHER	☐

TYPE OF INCIDENT Theft under $5,000.00

DATE OF ORIGINAL REPORT 07-09-16

BUS. PHONE (EXT./LOCAL) 905-561-4362

HOME PHONE (EXT./LOCAL) 905-555-0404

HAZARD ☐

SURNAME(OR NAME & TYPE OF BUSINESS) Creighton, Tom

ADDRESS 3001 Queens Rd., Hamilton, ON

At 17:00 hrs, Creighton returned to the locker room. The wallet was on the top shelf. He opened it and saw that there was no

money in it. He called the police from a pay phone.

Nothing else was stolen from the wallet. The other students reported stolen items from the locker room.

Investigation continues

HAZARD REMARKS (MUST BE COMPLETED IF HAZARD CHECKED)

REPORTING OFFICER (FULL NAME/RANK/No.) Joad, T. CST #1613

OTHER OFFICER(S) ATTENDING

DATE/TIME OF THIS REPORT O YR. 3|6 MO. E|P DAY 1|6

TIME 17:20

I.D. OFFICER REPORTING

PAGE No. 2

REPORT CHECKED BY (FULL NAME/RANK/No.)

CASE REASSIGNED TO

REPORT CHECKED BY (FULL NAME/RANK/No.)

INCIDENT STATUS (IF INVEST. COMP., CHECK SOLVED OR UNSOLVED)
INVEST. CONT. ☐   INVEST.COMP. ☐   SOLVED ☐   UNSOLVED ☐

BY **DATE** **INIT./DATE**

| STATS. CAN CLEARED BY | CHG. | OTHER | UNF. | INCIDENT CLASS | ADULTS M F | JUVENILES M F | INF. |
| DATA ENTRY | DATA VERIF. | DATA RECEIVED IN RECORDS | DATE CLEARED |

OFFICE USE ONLY

Sample 3: Disturbance

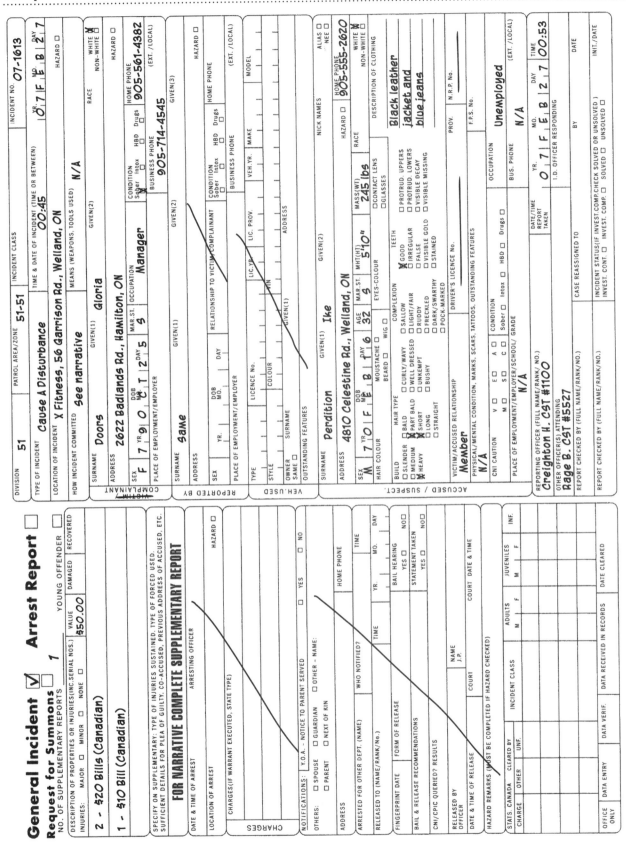

Sample 3 (Concluded)

Supplementary Report

INCIDENT NO. 07-1613

POLICE INFORMATION
- ACCUSED ☐
- (EXT./LOCAL) ☐
- HAZARD ☐

REFERENCE: COMPLAINANT ☒

HOME PHONE 905-561-4382

CHECK APPROPRIATE BOX
- ORIGINAL ☒
- ARREST ☐
- INCIDENT ☒
- VEHICLE ☐
- MISSING PERSON/ELOPEE ☐
- FRAUDULENT DOCUMENT ☐
- HOMICIDE/SUDDEN DEATH ☐
- OTHER ☐

SURNAME(OR NAME & TYPE OF BUSINESS)
Doors, Gloria

DIVISION: 51
PATROL AREA/ZONE: 51-51
INCIDENT CLASS

TYPE OF INCIDENT: **Cause A Disturbance**

DATE OF ORIGINAL REPORT: 07-02-27

BUS. PHONE (EXT./LOCAL) 905-714-4545

ADDRESS: 2622 Badlands Rd., Hamilton, ON

At 00:53 hrs, police attended at X Fitness, 56 Garrison Rd., regarding a disturbance. Upon arrival, officers were met by Gloria Doors, who told police that the suspect had left prior to police arrival. Doors reported the following to police:

She is the manager of X Fitness, a 24-hour gym. IKE PERDITION, age 32 yrs, has been a gym member for 10 months. During that time, he has told employees and other gym members about continuous domestic disputes with his girlfriend. He has described an unsettled relationship that includes frequent arguments to approximately 20 gym members and employees. Additionally, Perdition had told a number of people at the gym about his anger toward her and his desire to assault her. Doors could not provide verbatim threats that he has made, the names of the witnesses, or the specific times and dates of these occurrences.

Doors began her shift at 00:01 hrs. At 00:45 hrs, there were nine members in the gym working out. Perdition and a woman not known by Doors entered the gym. Perdition shouted at the woman, "I told you to shut up!" Perdition asked Doors to use the business phone. She refused. Perdition shouted, "Why not?" Doors told Perdition to leave. He shouted, "I want to use the phone!" The woman told Perdition, "Stop yelling."

Perdition shouted, "F___ off." He walked to the front entrance, shouting, "You're a b____" to the woman. Doors phoned the police. Perdition and the woman walked out of the gym, eastbound on Garrison Rd. Doors saw them arguing as they walked and lost sight of them. At 00:55 hrs, officers searched the area with negative results.

Investigation continues

PAGE NO. 1

DATE/TIME OF THIS REPORT: 0 YR 3 | F MO. E | B 2 DAY 7 | TIME 00:53

I.D. OFFICER REPORTING

REPORTING OFFICER (FULL NAME/RANK/NO.)
Creighton, H. CST #1100

OTHER OFFICER(S) ATTENDING
Rage, B. CST #5527

REPORT CHECKED BY (FULL NAME/RANK/NO.)
BY ____ DATE ____

REPORT CHECKED BY (FULL NAME/RANK/NO.)

CASE REASSIGNED TO

INCIDENT STATUS (IF INVEST. COMP. CHECK SOLVED OR UNSOLVED)
- INVEST. COMP. ☐ SOLVED ☐ UNSOLVED ☐
- INVEST. CONT. ☐ INVEST.COMP. ☐

INIT./DATE

HAZARD REMARKS (MUST BE COMPLETED IF HAZARD CHECKED)

STATS. CAN CLEARED BY	CHG.	OTHER	UNF.	DATA VERIF.	INCIDENT CLASS	DATA RECEIVED IN RECORDS	ADULTS M F	JUVENILES M F	INF.
OFFICE ONLY DATA ENTRY						DATE CLEARED			

Sample 4: Disturbance

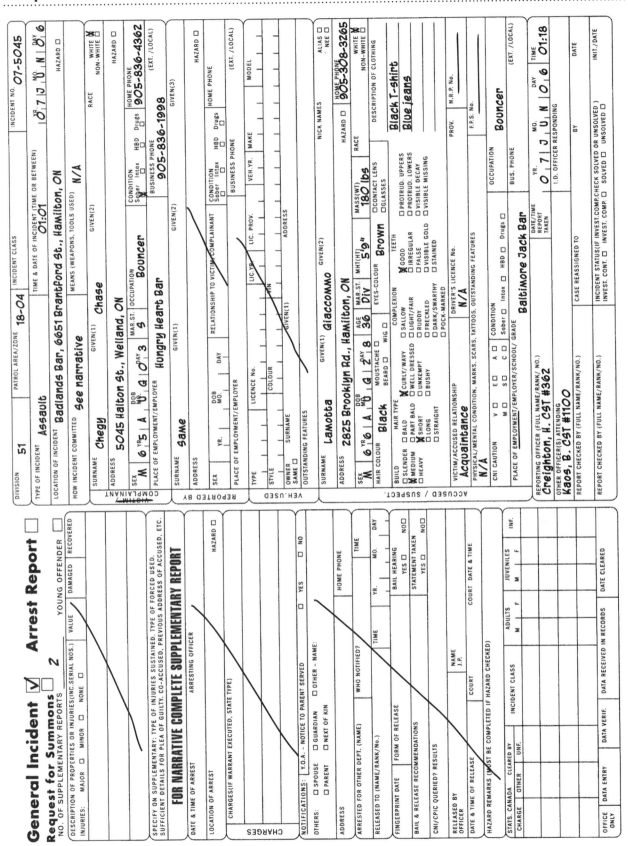

Sample 4 (Continued)

Supplementary Report

INCIDENT No. 07-5045

POLICE INFORMATION ☐
ACCUSED ☐ (EXT./LOCAL)
REFERENCE ☐ VICTIM ☒ COMPLAINANT
HOME PHONE 905-836-1998
HAZARD ☐

DIVISION 51
PATROL AREA/ZONE 18-04
TYPE OF INCIDENT Assault
INCIDENT CLASS
BUS. PHONE 905-836-4262 (EXT./LOCAL)
DATE OF ORIGINAL REPORT 07-06-06
ADDRESS 5045 Halton St., Welland, ON

CHECK APPROPRIATE BOX
ORIGINAL ☐ ARREST ☒ INCIDENT ☒ VEHICLE ☐
MISSING PERSON/ELOPEE ☐ FRAUDULENT DOCUMENT ☐ HOMICIDE/SUDDEN DEATH ☐ OTHER ☐

SURNAME(OR NAME & TYPE OF BUSINESS)
Chegy, Chase

At 01:18 hrs, police attended at BADLANDS BAR, 6651 Brantford St., Hamilton, ON, regarding a disturbance. Upon arrival, officers were met by CHASE CHEGY, the complainant in this matter. He reported the following:

Chegy is 37 years old and works as a bouncer at Hungry Heart Bar. He has known the suspect, Giaccommo Lamotta, for 12 years. They worked together for five years and they socialize frequently. Lamotta works as a bouncer at Baltimore Jack Bar. He is a former employee of Hungry Heart Bar, where he was fired six months ago for undisclosed reasons.

On 07-06-06, Chegy was not scheduled to work. At 21:00 hrs, he attended at Badlands Bar with a friend, Gloria Doors. Chegy frequently visits Badlands Bar and has socialized with Lamotta there on numerous occasions. Chegy and Doors sat at the bar. He consumed four beers between 21:00 – 01:00 hrs.

At 01:10 hrs, Lamotta entered Badlands Bar alone, via the side door. He walked directly to the bar and sat with Chegy. Lamotta was sober. Chegy saw no symptoms of intoxication. Lamotta sat on a bar stool to the left of Chegy while Doors sat on the right.

Lamotta did not order a beverage or food. He said to Chegy, "I thought I would find you here. I heard that you got me fired." Chegy responded, "Who told you that? They're lying." Lamotta answered, "Never mind who told me. What did you do to get me fired?" Chegy responded, "You're crazy. I told you I didn't do anything. You have no one to blame but yourself."

Lamotta punched Chegy with his left fist, striking Chegy's jaw. Chegy grabbed Lamotta's jacket. Lamotta grabbed Chegy's jacket. They pushed each other and exchanged profanities.

HAZARD REMARKS (MUST BE COMPLETED IF HAZARD CHECKED)

STATS. CAN CLEARED BY	CHG.	OTHER	UNF.	DATA VERIF.	INCIDENT CLASS	DATA RECEIVED IN RECORDS	ADULTS M F	JUVENILES M F	INF.
OFFICE USE ONLY	DATA ENTRY						DATE CLEARED		

DATE/TIME OF THIS REPORT YR 07 MO JUN DAY 06 TIME 01:18

REPORTING OFFICER (FULL NAME/RANK/No.) Creighton, H. CST #362
OTHER OFFICER(S) ATTENDING Kaos, B. CST #1100
REPORT CHECKED BY (FULL NAME/RANK/No.)
REPORT CHECKED BY (FULL NAME/RANK/No.)

CASE REASSIGNED TO

INCIDENT STATUS (IF INVEST. COMP. CHECK SOLVED OR UNSOLVED)
INVEST. CONT. ☐ INVEST.COMP. ☐ SOLVED ☐ UNSOLVED ☐

I.D. OFFICER REPORTING BY DATE INIT./DATE

PAGE No. 1

Sample 4   (Concluded)

Supplementary Report

CHECK APPROPRIATE BOX

ORIGINAL	☐	MISSING PERSON/ELOPEE	☒
ARREST	☐	FRAUDULENT DOCUMENT	☐
INCIDENT	☐	HOMICIDE/SUDDEN DEATH	☒
VEHICLE	☐	OTHER	☐

DIVISION	PATROL AREA/ZONE	INCIDENT CLASS		INCIDENT No.
51	18-04			07-5045

TYPE OF INCIDENT: Assault

REFERENCE: ~~COMPLAINT~~ ☒ COMPLAINANT   POLICE INFORMATION ☐   ACCUSED ☐ (EXT./LOCAL)

DATE OF ORIGINAL REPORT	BUS. PHONE (EXT./LOCAL)	HOME PHONE (EXT./LOCAL)
07-06-06	905-836-4262	905-836-1998

ADDRESS: 5045 Halton St., Welland, ON   HAZARD ☐

SURNAME(OR NAME & TYPE OF BUSINESS)

Chegy, Chase

Doors heard the conversation and saw Lamotta punch Chegy. She phoned the police with her cell phone and reported that a fight was in progress. Lamotta broke free of Chegy's grasp and walked out of the bar via the side door. His direction and method of travel were not seen.

Police arrived at 01:18 hrs. Chegy met the officers and reported the circumstances. He had a red mark on the right side of his jaw. He had suffered no other injuries. Witness statements were obtained from Doors and Chegy.

A search of the area was conducted with negative results.

Lamotta is 26 years old. He is 5'9", 180 lbs. He has short, curly brown hair and a goatee. He was wearing a navy blue T-shirt with red letters stating "Niagara X-Men Football" and blue jeans. Both Chegy and Doors can facially recognize him.

Investigation continues

HAZARD REMARKS	(MUST BE COMPLETED IF HAZARD CHECKED)		

	CHG.	OTHER	UNF.	INCIDENT CLASS	ADULTS M F	JUVENILES M F	INF.
STATS. CAN CLEARED BY							
OFFICE ONLY	DATA ENTRY	DATA VERIF.		DATA RECEIVED IN RECORDS	DATE CLEARED		

REPORTING OFFICER (FULL NAME/RANK/No.)
Creighton, H. CST #362

OTHER OFFICER(S) ATTENDING
Kaos, B. CST #1100   I.D. OFFICER REPORTING

DATE/TIME OF THIS REPORT	YR. 07	MO. JUN	DAY 06	TIME 01:18

CASE REASSIGNED TO	BY	DATE

REPORT CHECKED BY (FULL NAME/RANK/No.)

INCIDENT STATUS (IF INVEST. COMP., CHECK SOLVED OR UNSOLVED)
INVEST. CONT. ☐   INVEST. COMP. ☐   SOLVED ☐   UNSOLVED ☐

REPORT CHECKED BY (FULL NAME/RANK/No.)   INIT./DATE

PAGE No. 2

Sample 5: Belated Break and Enter

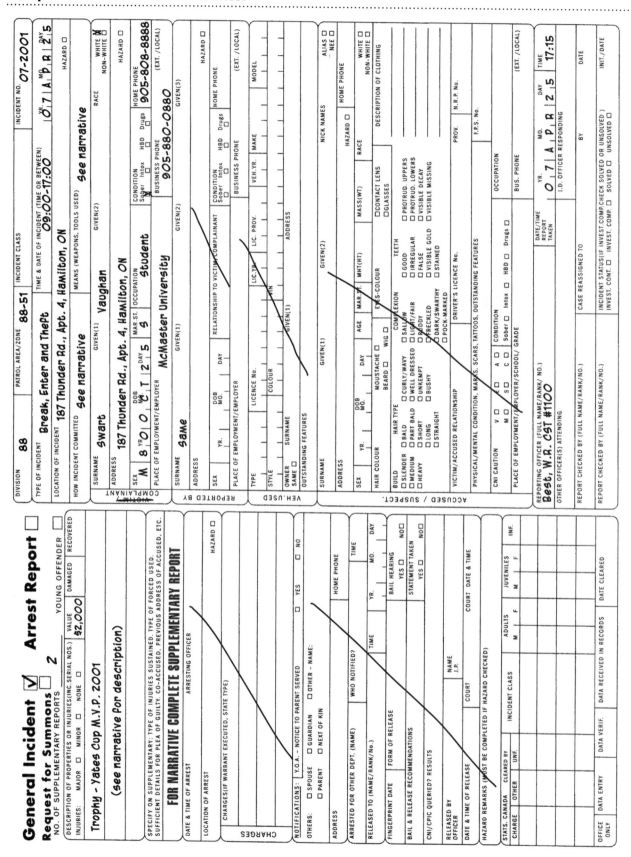

Sample 5   (Continued)

Supplementary Report

CHECK APPROPRIATE BOX

ORIGINAL	☐	MISSING PERSON/ELOPE ☒
ARREST	☐	FRAUDULENT DOCUMENT ☐
INCIDENT	☒	HOMICIDE/SUDDEN DEATH ☐
VEHICLE	☐	OTHER ☐

SURNAME(OR NAME & TYPE OF BUSINESS)

Swart, Vaughan

DIVISION **88**

PATROL AREA/ZONE **88-51**

INCIDENT CLASS

TYPE OF INCIDENT Break, Enter and Theft

DATE OF ORIGINAL REPORT **07-04-25**

BUS. PHONE **905-808-8888** (EXT./LOCAL)

HOME PHONE **905-880-0880** (EXT./LOCAL)

ADDRESS 187 Thunder Rd., Apt. 4, Hamilton, ON

REFERENCE

POLICE INFORMATION ☐
COMPLAINANT ☒   ACCUSED ☐
(EXT./LOCAL)

HAZARD ☐

INCIDENT NO. **07-2001**

At 17:15 hrs, 07-04-25, police attended at 187 Thunder Rd, Apt #4, Hamilton, regarding a belated break and enter. Upon arrival, the officer was met by Vaughan Swart, the complainant in this matter. He reported the following:

He is a 22-year-old third-year student at McMaster University. He lives at 187 Thunder Rd, Apt #4, Hamilton. He signed a rental agreement on 02-08-30 to live there. The building is owned by JAYGUN N. HUDDLE, 4382 Express St., Hamilton. Swart is the only occupant of the apartment.

Swart has been a member of the McMaster University football team for three years. On Nov. 15, 2001, he was awarded the following trophy:

- a brown 2 ft x 2 ft wooden base with a gold bowl attached to it

- a gold plate was attached to the front of the base with a printed inscription of:

"2001 YATES CUP MOST VALUABLE PLAYER"

"VAUGHAN SWART"

- the trophy is valued at $2,000

When he moved into his current apartment, he placed it on a wooden table situated in his living room. Hundreds of visitors have been in the apartment since then. The award has received national media coverage. Consequently, countless people have knowledge that Swart had possession of the trophy.

HAZARD
REMARKS   (MUST BE COMPLETED IF HAZARD CHECKED)

STATS. CAN CLEARED BY	CHG.	OTHER	UNF.	DATA VERIF.	INCIDENT CLASS	ADULTS		JUVENILES		INF.
						M	F	M	F	
OFFICE USE ONLY	DATA ENTRY				DATA RECEIVED IN RECORDS			DATE CLEARED		

REPORTING OFFICER (FULL NAME/RANK/NO.)

Best, W.R. CST #1100

OTHER OFFICER(S) ATTENDING

REPORT CHECKED BY (FULL NAME/RANK/NO.)

CASE REASSIGNED TO

REPORT CHECKED BY (FULL NAME/RANK/NO.)

DATE/TIME
OF THIS
REPORT

YR **07** MO. **APR** DAY **25** TIME **17:15**

I.D. OFFICER REPORTING

BY   DATE

INCIDENT STATUS (IF INVEST. COMP., CHECK SOLVED OR UNSOLVED)
INVEST. CONT. ☐ INVEST.COMP. ☐ SOLVED ☐ UNSOLVED ☐

INIT./DATE

PAGE NO. **1**

Sample 5   (Concluded)

Supplementary Report

CHECK APPROPRIATE BOX

ORIGINAL	☒	MISSING PERSON/ELOPE	☐
ARREST	☒	FRAUDULENT DOCUMENT	☐
INCIDENT	☒	HOMICIDE/SUDDEN DEATH	☐
VEHICLE	☐	OTHER	☐

DIVISION	PATROL AREA/ZONE	INCIDENT CLASS	INCIDENT No.
88	88-51		07-2001

REFERENCE	POLICE INFORMATION ☐
HOTLINE/COMPLAINANT ☒	ACCUSED ☐

TYPE OF INCIDENT
Break, Enter and Theft

DATE OF ORIGINAL REPORT	BUS. PHONE	(EXT./LOCAL)	HOME PHONE	(EXT./LOCAL)
07-04-25	905-808-8888		905-880-0880	

SURNAME(OR NAME & TYPE OF BUSINESS)
Swart, Vaughan

ADDRESS
187 Thunder Rd., Apt. 4, Hamilton, ON

HAZARD ☐

On 07-04-25, at 9:00 hrs, Swart left his apartment and locked the two doors, at the front and back of the apartment. He attended classes and remained at the university campus until 16:30 hrs.

At 17:00 hrs, he arrived at his residence. The back wooden door was open. The wood in the door and the frame was splintered near the door handle. A size 10 boot print was on the door. The pattern was visible and will be photographed by a Forensics Officer. After Swart entered the door, he walked through the kitchen and saw that nothing was missing or moved. He entered the living room and saw that the trophy was not on the table. He searched the entire apartment. Nothing else was stolen or moved. No lights or appliances had been turned on. The appearance of the apartment was the same as when he left at 09:00 hrs except for the missing trophy.

Swart phoned the police. Cst. W.R. Best arrived at 17:15 hrs. The damage and the boot print were seen by the officer. The Forensic unit was called to examine the crime scene.

Investigation continues

HAZARD REMARKS	(MUST BE COMPLETED IF HAZARD CHECKED)					

			ADULTS		JUVENILES		INF.
			M	F	M	F	

STATS. CAN CLEARED BY	CHG.	OTHER	UNF.	INCIDENT CLASS		
OFFICE ONLY	DATA ENTRY	DATA VERIF.	DATA RECEIVED IN RECORDS	DATE CLEARED		

REPORTING OFFICER (FULL NAME/RANK/NO.)
Best, W.R. Cst #1100

OTHER OFFICER(S) ATTENDING

REPORT CHECKED BY (FULL NAME/RANK/NO.)

REPORT CHECKED BY (FULL NAME/RANK/NO.)

CASE REASSIGNED TO

INCIDENT STATUS (IF INVEST. COMP., CHECK SOLVED OR UNSOLVED)
INVEST. CONT. ☐   INVEST.COMP. ☐   SOLVED ☐   UNSOLVED ☐

DATE/TIME OF THIS REPORT						
	YR	MO.		DAY		TIME
0 7	A P R	2 5	17:15

I.D. OFFICER REPORTING

BY	DATE

INIT./DATE

PAGE No. **2**

Sample 6: Alarm

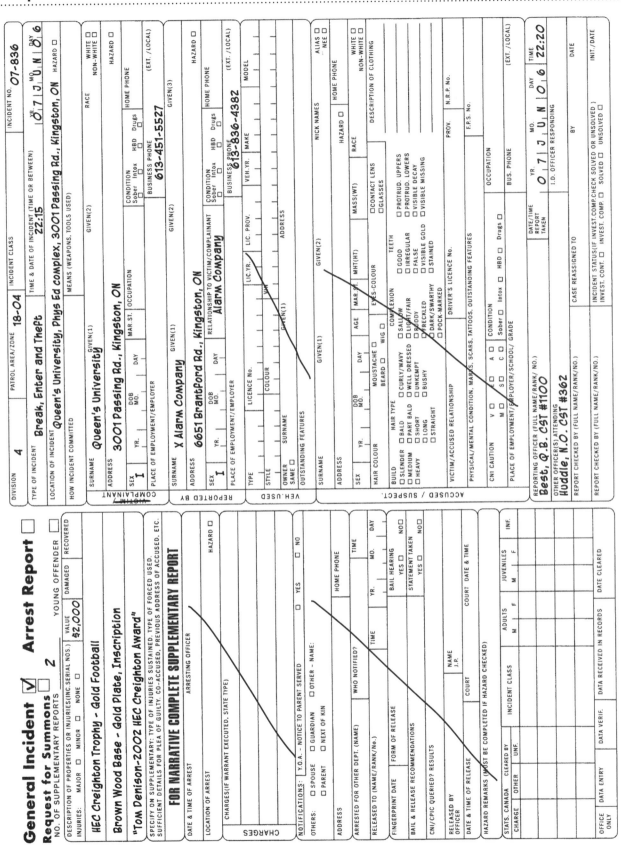

General Incident ☑   **Arrest Report** ☐
Request for Summons ☐   YOUNG OFFENDER ☐

NO. OF SUPPLEMENTARY REPORTS: 2

INJURIES: MAJOR ☐ MINOR ☐ NONE ☐   VALUE $2,000   DAMAGED ☐ RECOVERED ☐

DESCRIPTION OF PROPERTIES OR INJURIES(INC.SERIAL NOS.)

HEC Creighton Trophy – Gold Football

Brown Wood Base – Gold Plate, Inscription

"Tom Denison–2002 HEC Creighton Award"

SPECIFY ON SUPPLEMENTARY: TYPE OF INJURIES SUSTAINED. TYPE OF FORCED USED.
SUFFICIENT DETAILS FOR PLEA OF GUILTY. CO–ACCUSED, PREVIOUS ADDRESS OF ACCUSED, ETC.

FOR NARRATIVE COMPLETE SUPPLEMENTARY REPORT

DIVISION 4   PATROL AREA/ZONE 18-04   INCIDENT CLASS   INCIDENT NO. 07-836

TYPE OF INCIDENT: Break, Enter and Theft
TIME & DATE OF INCIDENT (TIME OR BETWEEN) 22:15   YR. 07 MO. JUN DAY 06   HAZARD ☐

LOCATION OF INCIDENT: Queen's University, Phys Ed complex, 3001 Passing Rd., Kingston, ON

HOW INCIDENT COMMITTED   MEANS (WEAPONS, TOOLS USED)

COMPLAINANT / VICTIM

SURNAME: Queen's University   GIVEN(1)   GIVEN(2)   RACE: WHITE ☐ NON-WHITE ☐

ADDRESS: 3001 Passing Rd., Kingston, ON   HAZARD ☐

SEX: I   YR. DOB MO. DAY   MAR.ST.   OCCUPATION   CONDITION Sober☐ Intox☐ HBD☐ Drugs☐   HOME PHONE

PLACE OF EMPLOYMENT/EMPLOYER   BUSINESS PHONE 613-451-5527   (EXT./LOCAL)

REPORTED BY

SURNAME: X Alarm Company   GIVEN(1)   GIVEN(2)   GIVEN(3)   HAZARD ☐

ADDRESS: 6651 Brantford Rd., Kingston, ON

SEX: I   YR. DOB MO. DAY   RELATIONSHIP TO VICTIM/COMPLAINANT: Alarm Company   CONDITION Sober☐ Intox☐ HBD☐ Drugs☐   HOME PHONE

PLACE OF EMPLOYMENT/EMPLOYER   BUSINESS PHONE 613-836-4382   (EXT./LOCAL)

VEH.USED

TYPE   LIC. PROV.   LIC.YR.   VEH.YR.   MAKE   MODEL

STYLE   COLOUR   GIVEN(1)

OWNER SAME ☐   SURNAME   ADDRESS

OUTSTANDING FEATURES

ACCUSED / SUSPECT

SURNAME   GIVEN(1)   GIVEN(2)   NICK NAMES   ALIAS ☐ NEE ☐

ADDRESS   HAZARD ☐   HOME PHONE

SEX   YR. DOB MO. DAY   AGE   MAR.ST.   MHT(HT)   MASS(WT)   RACE: WHITE ☐ NON-WHITE ☐

HAIR COLOUR   EYES-COLOUR   DESCRIPTION OF CLOTHING

BUILD: SLENDER ☐ MEDIUM ☐ HEAVY ☐   HAIR TYPE: BALD ☐ PART BALD ☐ SHORT ☐ LONG ☐ STRAIGHT ☐ CURLY/WAVY ☐ WELL DRESSED ☐ UNKEMPT ☐ BUSHY ☐   MOUSTACHE ☐ BEARD ☐ WIG ☐   COMPLEXION: SALLOW ☐ LIGHT/FAIR ☐ RUDDY ☐ FRECKLED ☐ DARK/SWARTHY ☐ POCK-MARKED ☐   TEETH: GOOD ☐ IRREGULAR ☐ FALSE ☐ VISIBLE GOLD ☐ DARK ☐   CONTACT LENS ☐ GLASSES ☐ PROTRUD. UPPERS ☐ PROTRUD. LOWERS ☐ VISIBLE DECAY ☐ VISIBLE MISSING ☐

VICTIM/ACCUSED RELATIONSHIP   DRIVER'S LICENCE No.   PROV.   N.R.P. No.

CNI CAUTION   V☐ A☐ M☐ S☐ C☐   CONDITION Sober☐ Intox☐ HBD☐ Drugs☐   OCCUPATION   F.P.S. No.

PHYSICAL/MENTAL CONDITION, MARKS, SCARS, TATTOOS, OUTSTANDING FEATURES

PLACE OF EMPLOYMENT/EMPLOYER/SCHOOL/ GRADE   BUS. PHONE   (EXT./LOCAL)

DATE/TIME REPORT TAKEN   YR. 07 MO. JUN DAY 06   TIME 22:20

REPORTING OFFICER (FULL NAME/RANK/NO.): Best, Q.B. CST #1100   I.D. OFFICER RESPONDING   DATE

OTHER OFFICER(S) ATTENDING: Huddle, N.O. CST #362   CASE REASSIGNED TO

REPORT CHECKED BY (FULL NAME/RANK/NO.)   INCIDENT STATUS(IF INVEST.COMP.CHECK SOLVED OR UNSOLVED)
INVEST. CONT. ☐ INVEST. COMP. ☐ SOLVED ☐ UNSOLVED ☐   BY   INIT./DATE

REPORT CHECKED BY (FULL NAME/RANK/NO.)   INVEST.CONT. ☐ INVEST. COMP. ☐ SOLVED ☐ UNSOLVED ☐

CHARGES

DATE & TIME OF ARREST   ARRESTING OFFICER

LOCATION OF ARREST   HAZARD ☐

CHARGES(IF WARRANT EXECUTED, STATE TYPE)

NOTIFICATIONS: Y.O.A. – NOTICE TO PARENT SERVED   YES ☐ NO ☐
OTHERS: SPOUSE ☐ GUARDIAN ☐ OTHER – NAME:
PARENT ☐ NEXT OF KIN ☐   YES ☐ NO ☐

ADDRESS   HOME PHONE

ARRESTED FOR OTHER DEPT. (NAME)   WHO NOTIFIED?   TIME   YR. MO. DAY   TIME

RELEASED TO (NAME/RANK/No.)   BAIL HEARING YES ☐ NO ☐

FINGERPRINT DATE   FORM OF RELEASE   STATEMENT TAKEN YES ☐ NO ☐

BAIL & RELEASE RECOMMENDATIONS

CNI/CPIC QUERIED? RESULTS   NAME J.P.

RELEASED BY OFFICER   COURT   COURT DATE & TIME

DATE & TIME OF RELEASE

HAZARD REMARKS (MUST BE COMPLETED IF HAZARD CHECKED)

STATS. CANADA   CLEARED BY   INCIDENT CLASS   ADULTS M F   JUVENILES M F   INF.

CHARGE OTHER UNF.   DATE CLEARED

OFFICE ONLY   DATA ENTRY   DATA VERIF.   DATA RECEIVED IN RECORDS

Sample 6   (Continued)

Supplementary Report

CHECK APPROPRIATE BOX

	ORIGINAL INCIDENT	☐	MISSING PERSON/ELOPEE	☒
	ARREST	☐	FRAUDULENT DOCUMENT	☐
	VEHICLE	☐	HOMICIDE/SUDDEN DEATH	☒
			OTHER	☐

SURNAME(OR NAME & TYPE OF BUSINESS)
Queen's University

DIVISION	PATROL AREA/ZONE	INCIDENT CLASS	REFERENCE	INCIDENT NO.
4	18-04		~~VICTIM~~/COMPLAINANT ☒	07-836

TYPE OF INCIDENT
Break, Enter and Theft

DATE OF ORIGINAL REPORT	BUS. PHONE (EXT./LOCAL)	HOME PHONE (EXT./LOCAL)
07-06-06	613-451-5527	

POLICE INFORMATION ☐
ACCUSED ☐
(EXT./LOCAL)
HAZARD ☐

ADDRESS
3001 Passing Rd., Kingston, ON

At 22:20 hrs, 07-06-18, police attended at the Queen's University Phys. Ed. Complex situated at 3001 Passing Rd., Kingston, ON, in response to a break and enter in progress. The premises is protected by the X Alarm Company. The alarm at the Phys. Ed. complex was activated at 22:15 hrs.

Upon arrival, officers searched the entrance of the building. Cst. Q.B. Best saw a shattered glass door on the east side of the building. This door was situated 30 metres from the front of the building, leading to an alleyway between the Phys. Ed. Complex and the Alumni Building. The view from Passing Rd. on the east side entrance was limited. The lighting in the alley was poor. A rock was seen on the floor inside the Phys. Ed. complex, one metre from the entrance, among the shattered glass. The front and back doors were locked. No cars were parked in front of the building. No persons were walking near the perimeter of the building.

Officers entered the building and searched the interior. No one was found inside.

A glass case in the front lobby was shattered. Nothing was inside the case. No footprints or other evidence was transferred near the shattered glass case. Management was notified following the search.

Gloria Doors, age 40 years, arrived at 22:30. Doors is the assistant athletic director. Her office is room PE 404; phone number 561-451-5527, ext. 4382. She reported the following:

She was the last person to leave the building on 07-06-18. At 19:30 hrs, she locked all the doors and set the alarm. The glass case in the lobby contained the Hec Creighton trophy, symbolic of the best Canadian university football player. The trophy was

HAZARD REMARKS	(MUST BE COMPLETED IF HAZARD CHECKED)				DATE/TIME OF THIS REPORT						

REPORTING OFFICER (FULL NAME/RANK/NO.)
Best, Q.B. Cst #1100

OTHER OFFICER(S) ATTENDING
Huddle, N.O. Cst #32

DATE/TIME OF THIS REPORT	YR	MO.	DAY	TIME
	07	JUN	06	22:20

PAGE No.
1

I.D. OFFICER REPORTING

	INCIDENT CLASS	DATA RECEIVED IN RECORDS		ADULTS M F	JUVENILES M F	INF.

REPORT CHECKED BY (FULL NAME/RANK/No.)

CASE REASSIGNED TO	BY	DATE

REPORT CHECKED BY (FULL NAME/RANK/No.)

INCIDENT STATUS (IF INVEST. COMP. CHECK SOLVED OR UNSOLVED)
INVEST. CONT. ☐   INVEST.COMP. ☐   SOLVED ☐   UNSOLVED ☐

INIT./DATE

STATS. CAN CLEARED BY	CHG.	OTHER	UNF.	DATA VERIF.
OFFICE ONLY	DATA ENTRY			DATE CLEARED

Sample 6   (Concluded)

Supplementary Report

	INCIDENT No.
	07-836

CHECK APPROPRIATE BOX

ORIGINAL	☒	MISSING PERSON/ELOPEE	☐
ARREST	☐	FRAUDULENT DOCUMENT	☐
INCIDENT	☒	HOMICIDE/SUDDEN DEATH	☐
VEHICLE	☐	OTHER	☐

DIVISION	PATROL AREA/ZONE	INCIDENT CLASS
4	18-04	

TYPE OF INCIDENT
Break, Enter and Theft

REFERENCE	POLICE INFORMATION ☐
VICTIM/COMPLAINANT ☒	ACCUSED ☐
	(EXT./LOCAL)

DATE OF ORIGINAL REPORT
07-06-06

BUS. PHONE (EXT./LOCAL)
613-451-5527

HOME PHONE

SURNAME(OR NAME & TYPE OF BUSINESS)
Queen's University

ADDRESS
3001 Passing Rd., Kingston, ON

HAZARD ☐

awarded to Tom Denison on November 23, 2006. The trophy was placed in the glass case on December 6, 2006. The case was
secured with a padlock. Doors has possession of the only key.

The trophy was described as follows:

- gold football, 36" in length, attached to a 3 ft x 3 ft brown wooden base

- the base had a gold plate attached to the front, with the following inscription in black printed letters:

"TOM DENISON"

"2006 HEC CREIGHTON AWARD"

The trophy is valued at $2,000. It had not been removed from the glass case since December 6.

Investigation continues

HAZARD REMARKS		(MUST BE COMPLETED IF HAZARD CHECKED)					

REPORTING OFFICER (FULL NAME/RANK/No.)
Best, Q.B. CST #1100

OTHER OFFICER(S) ATTENDING
Huddle, N.O. CST #32

DATE/TIME OF THIS REPORT

	YR	MO.	DAY		TIME
	0 7	J U N	0 6		22:20

I.D. OFFICER REPORTING

CASE REASSIGNED TO

REPORT CHECKED BY (FULL NAME/RANK/No.)   BY   DATE

REPORT CHECKED BY (FULL NAME/RANK/No.)

INCIDENT STATUS (IF INVEST. COMP., CHECK SOLVED OR UNSOLVED)
INVEST. CONT. ☐ INVEST. COMP. ☐ SOLVED ☐ UNSOLVED ☐

INIT./DATE

PAGE No.
2

STATS. CAN CLEARED BY	CHG.	OTHER	UNF.	INCIDENT CLASS	ADULTS M F	JUVENILES M F	INF.
OFFICE USE ONLY	DATA ENTRY	DATA VERIF.		DATA RECEIVED IN RECORDS	DATE CLEARED		

Sample 7: Missing Person

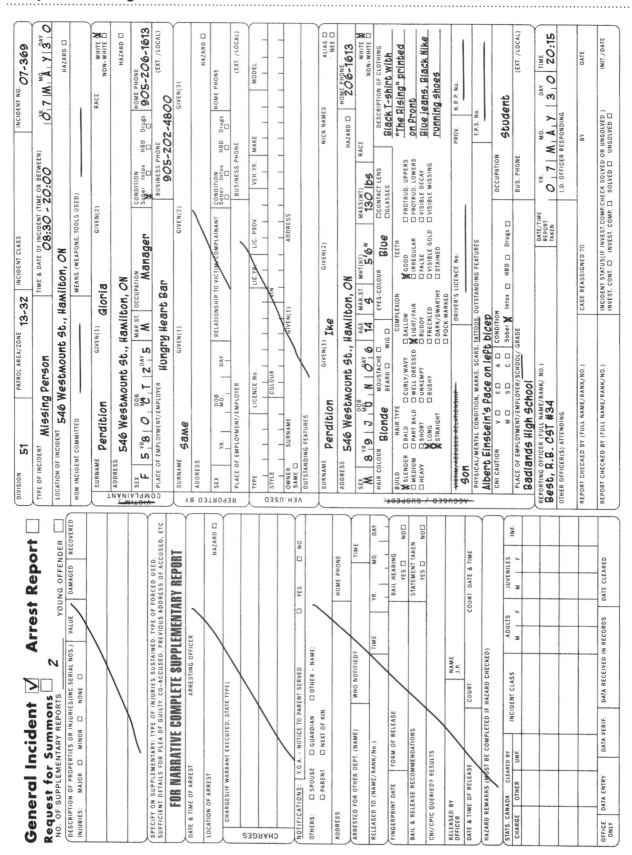

Sample 7   (Continued)

Supplementary Report

CHECK APPROPRIATE BOX

ORIGINAL ☒ | MISSING PERSON/~~ELOPE~~ ☒ | FRAUDULENT DOCUMENT ☐
ARREST ☐ | HOMICIDE/SUDDEN DEATH ☐
INCIDENT ☐ | OTHER ☐
VEHICLE ☐

SURNAME(OR NAME & TYPE OF BUSINESS)

Perdition, Gloria

DIVISION	PATROL AREA/ZONE	INCIDENT CLASS	INCIDENT No.
51	13-32		07-369

TYPE OF INCIDENT

Missing Person

REFERENCE | POLICE INFORMATION ☐
~~VICTIM~~/COMPLAINANT ☒ | ACCUSED ☐
(EXT./LOCAL)

DATE OF ORIGINAL REPORT | BUS. PHONE (EXT./LOCAL) | HOME PHONE (EXT./LOCAL) | HAZARD ☐

07-05-30 | **905-202-4800** | **905-206-1613**

ADDRESS

546 Westmount St., Hamilton, ON

At 20:15 hrs, police attended at 546 Westmount St., Hamilton, ON, regarding a missing person. Upon arrival, the officer was met by Gloria Perdition, who reported the following:

She is 45 years old and lives at 546 Westmount St. with her husband Larry (45) and two sons, Moe (16) and Ike (14). Both sons are students at Badlands High School.

Larry frequently abuses alcohol. He is routinely intoxicated and argues with the family when he is drunk. These episodes occur 4-5 times per week. Gloria has not seen Larry assault anyone.

Last night, Larry arrived home at 19:00 hrs. Gloria and her sons were home. She saw several symptoms of Larry's intoxication. A few minutes after Larry's arrival, he told Ike that he owed him $10 and he asked Ike why he neglected to cut the grass. Ike did not respond. Larry erupted in a profanity-laced tirade directed at Ike, calling him a "lazy degenerate." Ike went to his bedroom and stayed there for the remainder of the evening.

At 08:30 hrs, 07-05-30, Gloria ate breakfast with Ike and Moe while Larry slept. Gloria told Ike to return home immediately after school to cut the lawn. Ike answered, "Alright, get off my back." He immediately left the house, leaving Gloria and Moe in the kitchen.

Gloria believes that Ike walked to school alone. She does not know anyone who would have provided transportation. Moe arrived at the high school at 09:00 hrs and left at 16:30 hrs. He did not see Ike between those hours at school.

PAGE No. **1**

	DATE/TIME OF THIS REPORT		YR 0 , 7	MO M , A	DAY Y 3 , 0	TIME 20:15

I.D. OFFICER REPORTING

REPORTING OFFICER (FULL NAME/RANK/No.)

Best, R.B. CST #34

OTHER OFFICER(S) ATTENDING

REPORT CHECKED BY (FULL NAME/RANK/No.)	CASE REASSIGNED TO		BY	DATE
REPORT CHECKED BY (FULL NAME/RANK/No.)	INCIDENT STATUS (IF INVEST. COMP., CHECK SOLVED OR UNSOLVED) INVEST. CONT. ☐ INVEST.COMP. ☐ SOLVED ☐ UNSOLVED ☐		INIT./DATE	

HAZARD REMARKS | (MUST BE COMPLETED IF HAZARD CHECKED)

STATS. CAN CLEARED BY	CHG.	OTHER	UNF.	INCIDENT CLASS	ADULTS M F	JUVENILES M F	INF.
OFFICE ONLY	DATA ENTRY	DATA VERIF.		DATA RECEIVED IN RECORDS	DATE CLEARED		

Sample 7   (Concluded)

Supplementary Report

CHECK APPROPRIATE BOX

ORIGINAL	☒	MISSING PERSON/~~MINOR~~	☒
ARREST	☐	FRAUDULENT DOCUMENT	☐
INCIDENT	☐	HOMICIDE/SUDDEN DEATH	☐
VEHICLE	☐	OTHER	☐

DIVISION 51

PATROL AREA/ZONE 13-32

INCIDENT CLASS

REFERENCE ~~VICTIM~~/COMPLAINANT ☒

INCIDENT No. 07-369

POLICE INFORMATION ☐
ACCUSED ☐
HAZARD ☐

TYPE OF INCIDENT Missing Person

DATE OF ORIGINAL REPORT 07-05-30

BUS. PHONE (EXT./LOCAL) 905-202-4800

HOME PHONE (EXT./LOCAL) 905-206-1613

SURNAME(OR NAME & TYPE OF BUSINESS) Perdition, Gloria

ADDRESS 546 Westmount St., Hamilton, ON

Moe arrived home at 17:00 hrs. No one was home. Gloria arrived at 17:30 hrs. She called three of Ike's friends and was

informed that he was not with them. At 19:00 hrs, she drove in the surrounding area and did not see Ike. She called the police

at 20:00 hrs.

Ike's description is as follows:

— Male, white, 14 yrs, 5'6", 130 lbs, long, straight blonde hair, blue eyes

— wearing:

  — short sleeve black T-shirt with "THE RISING" printed in gold letters on the front;

  — blue jeans

  — black "NIKE" running shoes

  — tattoo of Albert Einstein's face on left bicep

— Ike has no history of leaving home for unexplained lengthy absences. He has not displayed unusual behaviour and there is

no evidence that he has threatened to harm himself in the past. There is no evidence of conflict with others.

Investigation continues

REPORTING OFFICER (FULL NAME/RANK/No.) Best, R.B. CST #34

OTHER OFFICER(S) ATTENDING

REPORT CHECKED BY (FULL NAME/RANK/No.)

REPORT CHECKED BY (FULL NAME/RANK/No.)

CASE REASSIGNED TO

DATE/TIME OF THIS REPORT
YR 07 MO. MAY DAY 30 TIME 20:15

I.D. OFFICER REPORTING

INCIDENT STATUS (IF INVEST. COMP. CHECK SOLVED OR UNSOLVED)
INVEST.COMP. ☐ SOLVED ☐ UNSOLVED ☐
INVEST. CONT. ☐ INVEST.COMP. ☐ SOLVED ☐ UNSOLVED ☐

BY   DATE

INIT./DATE

PAGE No. 2

HAZARD REMARKS (MUST BE COMPLETED IF HAZARD CHECKED)

| STATS. CAN CLEARED BY | CHG. | OTHER | UNF. | DATA VERIF. | INCIDENT CLASS | ADULTS M F | JUVENILES M F | INF. |
| OFFICE USE ONLY | DATA ENTRY | | | DATA RECEIVED IN RECORDS | DATE CLEARED | | | |

BELATED–PROACTIVE OCCURRENCE

Belated–proactive refers to an occurrence discovered by the police where the offender(s) is gone on arrival (GOA).

The best example is break, enter, and theft discovered by an officer during *property checks*, referring to general patrol and observation of commercial premises to determine whether the premises are secure or not. If an insecure premises is found, the place is searched for offenders. If the offenders are GOA, management is called and a before/during/after narrative is constructed by means of witness interviews and police observations.

The only difference between a belated–proactive and a belated–reactive GOR is the introduction. The other three stages are the same.

Belated–Proactive Template

At (time/date), Cst. (surname) was on routine, general patrol at (location: place, address) and found the building to be insecure (explain "insecure" point of entry). Officers entered the building. A search revealed negative results. The offender(s) were gone on arrival.

Management was notified. Mr./Mrs. (surname; position) arrived at (time). He/she reported the following:

_____

_____

_____

Events before	(same principles) who locked the building and when
Events during	(same principles) explained by post-offence observation (e.g., point of entry; missing items)
Events after	(same principles) forensic analysis witness interviews theories about offenders post-offence conduct and investigation

IN PROGRESS–REACTIVE OCCURRENCE

Emergency calls are considered to be "in progress" until investigation proves otherwise. Examples include:

- 911,
- unknown problem,
- interior alarm,
- domestic dispute,

- unwanted guest,
- disturbance, and
- weapons offences.

Offenders may be GOA or present upon arrival. If offenders are GOA and no arrest is made during the subsequent preliminary investigation, the same template is used as for a belated–reactive GOR, with one difference: events upon arrival are usually more extensive. This means that the introduction will likely be longer (e.g., injured persons, physical evidence found, crime scene appearance).

In Progress–Reactive Template

Response	At (time/date), police (or Cst. _____) responded to (place) regarding (specific radio broadcast call; e.g., 911).
Arrival	Upon arrival at (time), the following events were observed*: • who was present • who was injured • emergency services notified or present • what emergency services did and when • appearance of crime scene, with concrete explanation of what physical items were present and exactly where they were located • who secured and guarded the crime scene • who was interviewed first * before offence begins

In this type of occurrence, an arrest is the result in nearly all cases, and an Arrest Report will be required. See Chapter 8 for more information.

NOTES

1. D.R. Buchanan, "Enhancing Eyewitness Identification: Applied Psychology for Police Officers" (1985) 13, no. 4 *Journal of Police Science and Administration.*
2. S. Wood et al., *The World of Psychology*, 2nd Cdn ed. (Scarborough, ON: Prentice Hall, 1999) at 192–94.
3. Ibid.
4. Ibid.

CHAPTER 8
Arrest Report

INTRODUCTION

Arrest reports consist of the same cover page and narratives used in GORs. The same RSP system applies when writing them.

An arrest can occur:

- during the preliminary investigation (e.g., upon arrival at an "in-progress" call); or
- during a continued investigation (e.g., upon conclusion of the preliminary investigation).

An arrest report is needed any time a person is taken into *custody*, where the circumstances constitute an arrest or detention (by definition).

An *arrest* is defined as:

- actual restraint on a person's liberty, against that person's will; or
- physical custody of a person with the intent to detain.

Detention is defined as:

- deprivation of liberty by physical constraint; or
- the assuming of control over the movement of a person by demand or direction of a police officer; or
- a psychological compulsion existing within a person in the form of a perception that his/her freedom has been removed.[1]

An arrest report has the same elements as a GOR; it is composed of a cover page and a narrative written on Supplementary Reports. The cover page is the same one used for the GOR. In addition to the same fill-in-the-blanks information, the arresting officer must write:

- the accused person's information (name, D.O.B., address, phone, employment, description);
- offences committed (date and times included);
- time of arrest;
- time of release; and
- method of release.

The accuracy of these times is crucial with regard to the determination of *Charter* violations and the admissibility of evidence.

Arrests resulting in unconditional release (no charges) must be documented on an arrest report. An unconditional release does not negate the fact that an arrest occurred.

An arrest report narrative is often called a "summary," referring to the explanation of the evidence that establishes a *prima facie* case. In addition to being an organizational document, it has another major significance—the Crown Attorney who prosecutes the case will read it in court if the accused person enters a guilty plea.

The principles that govern an arrest report narrative are the same as those applicable to a GOR narrative, as explained in previous chapters. The primary aim of an arrest report narrative, as stated above, is to prove that a *prima facie* case exists. Achieving this objective automatically fulfills the second goal of proving that reasonable grounds existed to make the arrest.

If an arrest closes the investigation, the last sentence is either "Cleared by Charge" or "Cleared—Otherwise." "Cleared by Charge" is used when an Information will be laid. "Cleared—Otherwise" is used when the offender is released unconditionally (no Information laid).

ARREST AFTER ORIGINAL GOR

Template

Further to original report of Cst. (surname):

On (time/date), Cst. (surname) arrived at (place). Entry was gained by (explain in concrete language—e.g., prove consent; exigent circumstances; by Feeney warrant).

Upon entry (explain precise observation leading to discovery and identification of offender).

(Offender's surname) was told he/she was under arrest. He was informed of (explain the instructions—e.g., right to counsel; reason; caution). The accused stated (he understood or not—repetition needed).

He/she was searched (explain in concrete language how, where, and results). He was placed in the back of police vehicle number (___). (Explain the presence or absence of force used).

The following conversation occurred (verbatim).

Police left the (place) at (time) and arrive at (police station) at (time). The accused was escorted to (location of booking room).

Explain:
- additional search/seizure
- verbatim conservation re: lawyer
- additional verbatim conversation (e.g., exculpatory and inculpatory statements)
- time lodged in cell #___

The accused was released at (time) by means of (release document and officer's name).

IN PROGRESS–REACTIVE CALL

Template

Response	At (time/date), police (or Cst. _____) responded to (place) regarding (specific radio broadcast call, e.g., 911).

Arrival	Upon arrival at (time), the following events occurred:
	
	 The accused person (name and D.O.B.) was (location).
	
	 ▸ explain how he or she was arrested
	 ▸ explain verbatim conversation
	 ▸ use same guidelines from the "arrest after GOR" template
	 ▸ detail the instructions you communicated to the accused— whether or not he/she understood
	     ▸ search and seizure
	     ▸ exculpatory and inculpatory statements
	     ▸ time of departure from scene
	     ▸ time of arrival at police station
	     ▸ booking search and seizure
	     ▸ booking conversation
	     ▸ release: time and method

Before/During/After	Investigation revealed the following: (use the Before/During/After narrative system)

IN PROGRESS–PROACTIVE CALL

The best example of an in progress–proactive arrest is Impaired Driving.

Template

Accused person + position	On (date/time), the accused person was operating (description of motor vehicle) on (street, city) at (speed). The motor vehicle (describe manner of operation; i.e., if erratic, provide concrete explanation of erratic driving).
Police Action	Cst. (name) was operating (vehicle) on (location). He/she (describe actions, i.e., followed; stopped the accused) at (location). Cst. (name) (explain conduct; i.e., walked to the driver's door), and (explain conversation). The accused (describe symptoms, provide explanation of appearance and conduct). Cst. (name) arrested the accused at (time) and informed the accused of (reason, RTC, demand). ▸ time left scene ▸ time of arrival at police station ▸ time of blood alcohol test (BAT)/samples ▸ BAT test results

SUMMARY OF ARREST REPORT PRINCIPLES

Ensure that the following principles are observed when completing an arrest report.

1. Justify the arrest using concrete language.
2. Explain the exact length of time of custody.
3. Explain precisely what occurred during custody. The accused is in your care; what happens to him or her is your responsibility. Abstract language draws suspicion about the events that occurred during custody.

NOTE

1. *R v. Therens* (1985), 18 CCC (3d) 481 (SCC).

CHAPTER 9
Witness Statement

INTRODUCTION

A witness statement is a formal written record of a witness's observations relevant to an occurrence, representing the witness's potential or anticipated court testimony if a trial occurs.

There are several elements and general procedural rules that apply to witness statements.

1. *The document itself is not evidence that will be admitted in court to replace the witness's verbal testimony.*
   The witness must attend court and introduce his or her observations through sworn verbal testimony. The statement is a representation of what the witness is capable of testifying about. For prosecution purposes, the only thing that matters is what the witness says during testimony at the trial.

2. *Rules of evidence govern the extent and nature of the content of a witness statement.*
   The scope of a witness's court testimony is governed by a complex series of laws called *rules of evidence*. They are explained in the supplementary textbook, *Criminal Investigation*. Because a witness statement is a representation of the witness's potential testimony, the statement's content is governed by the same rules of evidence. The four prominent rules of evidence are:
   a. Observations perceived by one's own sense are admissible, if they are relevant.
   b. Hearsay is generally inadmissible.
   c. Opinions are generally inadmissible.
   d. Bad character evidence is generally inadmissible.

   This means that the central focus of the content, generally, is about what the witness saw and what the witness heard the offender say, but not what he or she was told or did not see.

3. *The hearsay, opinion, and bad character rules of evidence have exceptions.*
   The phrase "generally inadmissible" means that usually a witness cannot testify about a certain type of evidence but some exceptions exist. Consequently, these three types of evidence are included in a witness

statement when the circumstances make it likely that they will be admissible during the trial. For example, the most notable exception to the hearsay rule was established by the Supreme Court of Canada in *R v. Khan* (1990).[1] According to *Khan*, hearsay is admissible when the prosecutor proves that it is "necessary and reliable." Specifically, this refers to:

- an incompetent child witness,
- prior inconsistent statements, or
- a witness's death prior to trial.

There are several non-expert opinions that are admissible, including a person's age, distance, speed, facial recognition, and intoxication.

4. *The witness dictates the statement and the officer writes it.*
There are three reasons why a witness cannot write his or her own statement:

  a. the witness will not know the rules of evidence;
  b. the witness will not structure the content properly or precisely; and
  c. credibility cannot be evaluated accurately when a witness simply writes his or her own statement without verbalizing it to the officer.

The recording officer is the recipient of hearsay evidence. He or she cannot testify about the content reported by the witness, except:

- when a hearsay exception is permitted by the trial judge, allowing its admissibility; and
- at bail hearings and *ex parte* hearings, where hearsay is always admissible.

5. *Officers must write their own witness statements according to the same rules of evidence.*
There are three common observations that are perceived by an officer's own senses:

  a. being an eyewitness to an offence—Impaired Driving and Cause a Disturbance are examples of offences most commonly witnessed by patrol officers;
  b. verbal or written statements made by an offender; and
  c. finding and seizing physical evidence.

6. *Written statements are written in the first person.*
This means that the pronoun "I" is used to designate the observer.

7. *A witness statement may be used to refresh memory before a trial.*
Any witness (citizen or police officer) may review his or her statement prior to testifying in court if the statement is contemporaneous, meaning that it was written shortly after the observation and it was read over and signed by the witness.

Accordingly, a witness statement serves four purposes:

  a. it informs the Crown Attorney of a witness's anticipated evidence;
  b. it is a formal record of the reasonable grounds that justified police decisions and actions;

c. it provides memory recall assistance; and

d. it is a legal remedy for prosecution problems including hostile witnesses, incompetent witnesses, and witnesses unable to testify.

FORMAT

There is no specific legal form that must be used for a witness statement. There are three formats that may be used:

1. a formal witness statement designed by a police service,
2. an officer's personal notebook, or
3. ordinary lined paper.

A witness statement is composed of a heading and the narrative. The heading is a simple sentence that introduces the witness's name. It may be written either as:

- "(Witness's name) will say:" or
- "The anticipated evidence of (witness's name):".

The narrative begins after the heading. The same RSP principles apply to witness statements as to other narratives previously discussed.

Relevance in statement writing refers to a focus on three primary areas:

1. FII of the offence,
2. rules of evidence, and
3. factors affecting observation and credibility.

The structure of a witness statement is the same as for other narratives. There are four stages that chronologically order the information—an introduction followed by events before, during, and after the crime. During each stage, precision is imperative.

Template

> (Name of witness) will say:
>
> I am (____) years old. I live at (address) with (names). I am employed at (organization) where I hold the position of (occupation).
>
> On (day, date, time) I was (explain activity leading to the observation).

Writing the "Introduction"

The first stage is the witness's brief personal resume, wherein the witness introduces him or herself by:

- age;
- address;
- marital status;
- children, or occupants of house; and
- occupation, employer and position held. If no occupation, state the source of income (e.g., pension recipient).

Writing the Events "Before the Occurrence"

Explain the witness's relevant activities preceding the offence. The starting point may be the morning of the offence or further in the past if relevant circumstances occurred. This stage emphasizes and includes:

- evidence proving the offender's identity, including any extent of familiarity with the offender, such as the length of time and the specific nature of the familiarity or relationship;
- a description of the offender—if the familiarity with the offender was minimal, the witness's capability of facially recognizing the offender;
- circumstances proving the offender's planning and intent, including the motive that developed;
- conversations with potential suspects;
- circumstances that create mere suspicion; and
- witness's activities on the offence date relevant to strength of observation and credibility, including:
  - work hours;
  - presence or absence of alcohol/substance consumption; and
  - specific circumstances that may have drawn attention to the crime location prior to the offence occurring.

Writing the Events "During the Occurrence"

- Eyewitness observation of *actus reus.*
- Concrete language only.
- Observations include:
  - time when observation began;
  - witness's location/position;
  - offender's location/position;
  - type of view (obstructed or clear);
  - noise level;
  - verbatim statements made by the offender;
  - offender's description;
  - descriptions of physical items involved;
  - manner in which items were used;
  - capability of facial recognition;
  - capability of voice recognition;
  - duration of the observation; and
  - stress level (witness's perception of risk to himself or herself).

Writing the Events "After the Occurrence"

After the *actus reus* concludes, a number of circumstances constitute evidence that proves the offender committed the offence. This stage of the statement begins upon completion of the offence and continues until the offender's arrest. Consequently, the reported circumstances may occur shortly after the offence or after significant time lapses. In some cases, a witness statement will be composed solely of this final state, where the witness makes observations or communicates with the offender after the offence but saw nothing relevant before or during the offence. The majority of police officer statements are usually concentrated on this stage because most police observations occur reactively rather than proactively.

The relevant facts pertaining to this stage are observations of post-offence conduct, including:

- verbal and written statements made by the offender to anyone (police or citizen), at any time after the *actus reus* until the matter is disposed of in court. As always, offenders' statement are written verbatim. The following facts accompany each verbatim statement:
    - time and date of the statement;
    - place where the statement was made;
    - persons present during the statement; and
    - an explanation of why and how the offender and witness met to have the conversation (if the statement was made to a citizen). The offender's description is included, especially if the statement was made on a day subsequent to the offence date;
- direction and means of travel;
- items that the offender possessed upon departure from the crime scene or at any time after the offence was committed;
- description of items stolen or that were found by witnesses;
- description of the appearance of the crime scene or other relevant places when observation were made (if the witness arrived after the *actus reus* concluded);
- all times, dates, places, and names of others present during observations made on days subsequent to the offence or on the offence date;
- police statements that include:
    - time of arrival;
    - description of crime scene appearance;
    - names of persons present, including their activities;
    - circumstances relevant to crime scene protection and contamination;
    - searches, including:
        - target (person or place);
        - authorization (with or without a warrant, or by consent);
        - persons present;
        - scope of and activities during the search;
        - outcomes; and
        - if seizure made, precise description of the item(s) and its position and location;
- verbatim statements made by offenders; and
- potentially admissible hearsay, opinion, and bad character evidence.

Finalizing the Witness Statement

Upon completion of a statement dictated by a witness, follow the procedures below.

1. Allow the witness to read it.
2. If alterations are made, the witness writes his or her initials next to them.

3. If multiple pages are written, the witness writes his or her initials at the bottom of each page, as close as possible after the last word on each page.

4. The witness signs the statement by writing his or her signature as close as possible after the last word.

5. The officer signs the statement after the witness's signature.

6. Record the following on the statement and in your notebook:
   - the time the interview began,
   - the time the interview concluded,
   - the location, and
   - persons present.

Not all witnesses will have relevant observations during the three stages of an offence. Some witnesses may have made relevant observations during only one stage, such as before or after the offence. As stated, police witness statements usually reflect events that occurred after the *actus reus* ended.

SAMPLE: CITIZEN WITNESS STATEMENT

MEZZO MATTO WILL SAY:

I am 25 years old. I live at 2622 Barton Street, Welland, with my parents. I am employed at Niccolo's Department Store, 4424 Machiavelli Ave., Welland, where I hold the position of security guard/retail investigator.

On July 1, 2007, I was working the 10:00 a.m. to 6 p.m. shift, assigned to internal store patrol.

At 1:50 p.m., I saw a male person, who later identified himself to me as Sempro Adruggato, enter the store via the front entrance. I was standing in aisle #6 at the time, 20 metres from the front entrance, and I had a clear view of him. The reason I noticed him was that I recognized him as a past customer. He has been in the store several times in the past but he has never purchased items.

I followed Adruggato for about ten minutes. He walked down four aisles. He looked at several items and put them all back on the shelves. He repeatedly looked from side to side while he was shopping, which heightened my suspicion.

At 2:00 p.m., Adruggato entered the electronics aisle. I stood 20 metres away pretending to shop while I had a clear view of his position. As he stood in front of a CD display, I saw him pick up a CD with "The Rising" printed on the front. He looked to his left and then to his right. He placed the CD into his left jacket pocket. He walked to the front entrance and exited the store without paying for the CD.

I followed him to the parking lot and I stopped him. I had not lost sight of him from the time of the offence until the time of apprehension. I identified myself by name and told him that I was a "store security guard." I said to him, "You're under arrest for theft under $5,000." I read the right to counsel to him from my notebook. I asked him, "Do you understand?"

He replied, "Ya. I don't need a lawyer." I read the caution to him from my notebook and asked, "Do you understand?" He replied, "Ya." I then said to him, "Let's go to the security office inside." Adruggato put his hand in his left jacket pocket, removed the CD, gave it to me and said, "Sorry for stealing it. Can I pay for it now?" I replied, "Come on, let's go," and we walked inside to the security office.

Upon arrival at 2:05 p.m., I phoned the police. I asked for identification. He produced a driver's licence with the name Sempro Adruggato on it. I initialled the plastic cover of the CD. The CD had a $25 sticker on the front. I wrote my note at this time.

At 2:15 p.m., Cst. Huddle arrived at the office. I showed Cst. Huddle my notes and I verbally explained that I saw Adruggato take the CD and leave the store without paying for it. I gave the CD to Cst. Huddle.

I heard Cst. Huddle tell Adruggato, "You're under arrest for theft under $5,000." Cst. Huddle read the right to counsel from a notebook and asked, "Do you understand?" Adruggato replied, "Ya, I already told him I don't want a lawyer." Cst. Huddle read the caution from a notebook and asked, "Do you understand?" Adruggato answered, "Ya, I already told him I understand."

Cst. Huddle asked Adruggato, "Why did you steal it?" Adruggato answered, "Springsteen is the best musician, 'The Rising' is the best CD, so I stole it."

Cst. Huddle asked him questions to complete an arrest report. At 2:35 p.m., Cst. Huddle gave Adruggato an Appearance Notice. Adruggato signed. They both left.

SAMPLE: POLICE WITNESS STATEMENT (REACTIVE)

CST. N. HUDDLE WILL SAY:

I am a member of the Niagara Regional Police Service where I hold the rank of constable. I am assigned to the uniform branch of 51 Division.

On July 1, 2007, I was working the 7 a.m. to 7 p.m. shift assigned to general patrol duties. As a result of information received from a radio broadcast, I attended at Niccolo's Department Store, 4424 Machiavelli Ave., Welland, at 2:15 p.m. I walked to the security office. Two men were in the office. I identified myself to both men.

Mezzo Matto introduced himself. He gave me a driver's licence with the name Sempro Adruggato on it. Matto gave me a notebook. I read the notes in it. Additionally, he informed me about certain information. Matto gave me a CD with "The Rising" printed on the front. A $25 sticker was on the cover. I saw the initials "MM" on the cover. I seized the CD.

Based on the information I learned, I told Adruggato that he was under arrest for theft under $5,000. I read the right to counsel from my notebook and I asked him, "Do you understand?" Adruggato replied, "Ya, I already told him I don't want a lawyer." I read the caution from my notebook and I asked him, "Do you understand?" He replied, "Ya, I already told him I understand."

I asked Adruggato, "Why did you steal it?" Adruggato replied, "Springsteen is the best musician, 'The Rising' is the best CD, so I stole it."

I asked him questions to complete an arrest report. I completed an Appearance Notice. I explained it to Adruggato and asked him to sign. He signed it and I gave him a copy of it.

I left the store at 2:35 p.m. and arrived at 51 Division at 2:43 p.m. I initialled the cover of the CD and placed it in Locker #4 in the property room.

At 2:51 p.m., I wrote notes relevant to this incident.

SAMPLE: POLICE WITNESS STATEMENT (PROACTIVE)

CST. H. CREIGHTON WILL SAY:

I am a member of the Niagara Regional Police Service, where I hold the rank of constable. I am assigned to the uniform branch of 51 Division.

On July 4, 2007, I was working the 7 p.m. to 7 a.m. shift, assigned to general patrol duties. At 10:15 p.m., I was parked at a gas station situated on the southwest corner of King St. and Lincoln St. I had completed a General Occurrence Report and was preparing to leave that location. As I looked at the traffic on King St., I saw a white BMW travelling north on King St. The car passed First St. and travelled toward Lincoln St. The speed of the car drew my attention to it. The posted speed on King St. is 50 km/h. The car's speed was faster than the other traffic in my view. In my opinion, the BMW was travelling at a speed beyond the posted speed limit.

The traffic light facing northbound traffic on King St. was red. I saw the BMW fail to stop for the red light and travel through the intersection, continuing north on King St. I was parked about 20 metres from the northbound lane. My view was unobstructed. The weather was clear and the roads were dry.

I turned left onto King St. and travelled north, following the BMW. When I arrived at a distance of about 10 metres behind the BMW, I saw the plate number—Ontario CLTS 424. The driver was a male person. He was the lone occupant.

I activated the roof lights of the cruiser. The distance between my cruiser and the BMW remained the same for about two blocks. The cruiser speedometer read 70 km/h.

The BMW crossed the midline of the roadway and travelled partially in the southbound lane for about 50 metres. The car returned to the northbound lane. I saw the brake lights activate. The car stopped near the east curb of King St, about 10 metres south of Division St.

I walked to the driver's window. The window was down. The driver was male, white, about 25 years old, short black hair, black goatee, an earring in his left ear in the shape of a cross, and wearing a purple t-shirt. The driver asked, "What's the problem?" as I leaned toward the driver's door. I smelled the odour of an alcoholic beverage on his breath. His eyes were red. His speech was slurred as he asked the question. I responded by asking him to produce his driver's licence, ownership, and insurance. He searched his front left pant pocket, then his right front pant pocket. He said something that I did not understand. He reached into his left back pant pocket and removed a brown wallet. He opened it and I illuminated it with my flashlight. He searched through the wallet. I saw a driver's licence three times in a plastic folder while he searched. He then removed the driver's licence and gave it to me. The name on the driver's licence was Jake Umbriaggo, D.O.B. 80–6–06, 6651 Orchard Ave., Welland.

I told Umbriaggo to get out of the car. He opened the driver's door. He lifted his left leg to leave the car and fell to the ground. I helped him stand. He was unbalanced as I held his left arm.

I told him he was under arrest for impaired driving. I walked with him to my cruiser and I searched him. Upon completion of the search, he entered the back of my cruiser. I entered the front of the cruiser and read the right to counsel from my notebook. I asked, "Do you understand?" He replied, "Ya, I don't want a lawyer." I read the caution to him from my notebook. I asked him if he understood. Umbriaggo replied, "Ya."

I then read the demand for breath samples to him and asked if he understood. He replied, "What does that mean?" I explained the following: "It means I am demanding that you take a Breathalyzer test and provide two breath samples so that your blood alcohol content can be determined. You have to provide the breath samples. You have no choice. If you refuse, you will be charged with Refusing to Comply with the Demand. Do you understand?" He replied, "Ya, I'll take the test. I'm not drunk. I only had a couple of beers."

I asked the dispatcher to send a tow truck. At 10:23 p.m., I left the scene of the arrest and drove to the police station. En route, Umbriaggo said, "I only had a couple of beers. I'm not that drunk." His speech was slurred. He then mumbled something that I did not understand. I did not respond. No further conversation occurred.

We arrived at the police station at 10:27 p.m. We entered past the security guard and I led Umbriaggo to the booking room. I asked him questions to complete an arrest report.

At 10:32 p.m., I led Umbriaggo to the Breathalyzer room. I introduced him to Cst. E. Sky and I left the room.

At 10:34 p.m., I wrote notes in my notebook. I completed reports afterward. I returned to patrol at 11:15 p.m.

NOTES

1. *R v. Khan* (1990), 59 CCC (3d) 92 (SCC).

CHAPTER 10
Crown Brief

INTRODUCTION

After an arrest is made, the accompanying arrest report is written as soon as practicable. It is submitted during the same tour of duty in which the arrest is made; it is not submitted on a later date. Initially, the arrest report serves an organizational tool. It provides a record for the respective police service. If a charge is laid, an additional report called a Crown Brief is required.

DEFINITION

A Crown Brief is a book that explains all of the evidence that is available and that can be introduced at a trial to prove a formal allegation. It is written after an Information is laid to formally charge an accused person(s). Conversely, a Crown Brief is not required if no charges are laid.

Crown Briefs are written by the police; usually the arresting officer has the onus of writing it. After the Crown Brief is completed, it is submitted to the Crown Attorney, who develops the prosecution strategy from it. In other words, the Crown Attorney relies exclusively on the Crown Brief to determine how a *prima facie* case will be established at a trial.

Consequently, Crown Briefs are the primary means of communication between the arresting officer and the Crown Attorney. In some cases, they are the only means of communication. The extent of the relevance, precision, and accuracy of the evidence conveyed in a Crown Brief largely determines the success or failure of a prosecution.

Additionally, the Crown Brief is the Crown Attorney's primary means of making **disclosure** to the defence/accused person. The Crown has the onus to provide disclosure to the accused after an Information has been laid. Failure to provide disclosure may constitute a violation of section 7 of the *Charter*. Therefore, an incomplete Crown Brief may be equivalent to improper disclosure, which may result in a *Charter* violation.

CONCEPT OF DISCLOSURE

A Crown Brief should be prepared in a manner that fulfils the Supreme Court of Canada's guidelines relating to proper disclosure, found in *R v. Stinchcombe* (1991).[1] Disclosure is defined as "the divulging of all relevant material by the Crown to the accused/defence, after an Information has been laid." A Crown Brief must contain all relevant material because it is the primary means of providing disclosure. Relevant material is defined as:

- Any information that is of "some use." The defence determines what information is of some use, not the Crown.
- Inculpatory and exculpatory evidence. Evidence obtained by the police that benefits the defence cannot be concealed by the Crown.
- All statements obtained from persons by police officers, whether or not the person will be compelled to court by the Crown as a witness. The statement of a person who will not be subpoenaed by the Crown cannot be concealed by the Crown.
- The name, address, and occupation of persons from whom no statement was taken. If the person was interviewed by an officer and the person's observations were recorded in the officer's notebook, the officer's notes must be disclosed. The only exception is the identity of a confidential informant; however, this exception is subject to review by the trial judge.

Initial disclosure should be made before the accused enters a plea. Consequently, the Crown Brief must be submitted to the defence before the accused person's first appearance in court.

The Crown's obligation of disclosure does not end after the initial disclosing of the Crown Brief. After the initial Crown Brief is submitted to the defence, any relevant material that is subsequently obtained by the police must also be disclosed to the defence. In other words, the Crown cannot conceal any evidence obtained before or after the Information is sworn and the Crown Brief is prepared because the Crown's disclosure obligation remains continuous until the trial.

STRUCTURE

A Crown Brief is composed of the following five parts:

- cover page
- introduction page
- witness list
- summary
- witness statements.

Cover Page

The title of the case is the only information typed on this page. The title is simply *Regina vs. (accused's person's name).*

TEMPLATE

Regina
vs.
(accused's name)

EXAMPLE

Regina vs. Jack Umbriaggo	

Introduction Page

Five facts are listed on this one-page document:

1. short-form name of the offence, *Criminal Code* section number, and statute;
2. offence date;
3. accused person's name, address, and date of birth;
4. offence location; and
5. name of the arresting officer or the officer-in-charge of the case.

TEMPLATE

OFFENCE:	(name of offence and section/statute)
OFFENCE DATE:	(date of offence)
ACCUSED PERSON:	(name, address, D.O.B.)
OFFENCE LOCATION:	(place)
OFFICER-IN-CHARGE:	(name of investigating officer)

EXAMPLE

OFFENCE:	Robbery Section 344 *Criminal Code*
OFFENCE DATE:	June 6, 2007
ACCUSED PERSON:	Jake Umbriaggo 3001 Denison Rd., Welland, Ontario L0B 2R6 D.O.B. 69–08–02
OFFENCE LOCATION:	City of Welland
OFFICER-IN-CHARGE:	Cst. H. Creighton

Witness List

The arresting officer has the onus of composing the witness list. The purpose of the witness list is to reveal and identify all persons who will be subpoenaed by the police and called by the Crown to testify at the trial. It must list sufficient witnesses to prove each fact-in-issue of the offence alleged on the Information, beyond **reasonable doubt**.

Witnesses will include citizens and police who have made relevant observations or who have relevant documents or items to introduce at the trial. Sufficient information is needed to find each witness and serve him or her with a subpoena—name, home address, and work address. A synopsis that briefly describes the witness's employment and the nature of his or her anticipated evidence may be printed next to the witness's name.

TEMPLATE

WITNESS LIST	SYNOPSIS
1. Witness name address contact information	brief, one sentence summary of witness's role
2. Witness name address contact information	same

EXAMPLE

WITNESS LIST	SYNOPSIS
1. Gloria Doors 1000 Thunder Rd. Welland, Ontario L2C 3T7 or c/o First National Bank 2000 Benoit St. Welland, Ontario L3D 4V8	bank manager; witnessed robbery
2. Claire Matto 5000 Grabell Rd. Welland, Ontario L4E 5X9 or c/o First National Bank 2000 Benoit St. Welland, Ontario L3D 4V8	bank teller; had gun pointed at her and was robbed of money

Summary

A summary is a narrative that explains how the evidence obtained during the investigation proves that the offender named on the Information committed the offence alleged on the Information. When an accused person enters a guilty plea, the summary represents the Crown Attorney's primary means of communication to the trial judge. After a guilty plea is entered, the Crown Attorney reads the summary to the trial judge. Consequently, a summary must fulfill the following objectives:

- it must unequivocally establish a *prima facie* case; and
- it must prove all the facts-in-issue of the offence alleged on the Information beyond reasonable doubt.

Consequently, the facts-in-issue that constitute the offence must be identified before writing the summary. Relevant content is that which proves the facts-in-issue. Therefore, the summary must include:

- the constant facts-in-issue:
  - identity of accused
  - date and time of offence
  - location of offence;
- the facts-in-issue that constitute the *actus reus*. These are determined by analysis of the relevant sectionin the *Criminal Code* where the offence is found; and
- *mens rea.*

A summary has four stages:

1. introduction
2. events before the offence
3. events during the offence
4. events after the offence.

TEMPLATE

The charge(s) of (name of offence(s)) arise from an incident that occurred at (place), situated at (address, city) on (day, date, time).

The accused person in this matter is (accused's name, D.O.B., address).

The victim/complainant in this matter is (name, D.O.B., address). The circumstances of the offence are as follows:

On (date/time), (explain the first relevant event **before** the crime. In chronological order, explain the remaining relevant events that occurred before the offence).

On (date/time), (explain the first relevant event **during** the crime. In chronological order, explain the remaining relevant events that occurred during the offence).

On (date/time), (explain **post-offence** conduct and investigation in chronological sequence. Includes the time/date/place of the arrest, the Charter instructions and caution communicated to the accused, what police station he/she was detained at, and whether the accused confessed or not).

On (date/time), (explain the method of release, result of a bail hearing, or how the accused was compelled to court).

EXAMPLES

Introduction

The first stage of the summary introduces the complainant, the accused person, the offence date/time, and the offence location.

> The charge of robbery in this matter arises from an incident that occurred at the First National Bank, situated at 2000 Benoit Street in the city of Welland, Ontario, on Tuesday, June 6, 2007, at 3:00 p.m.
>
> The accused person charged with robbery in this matter is:
>
> Jake Umbriaggo, D.O.B. 69–08–02, 3001 Denison Rd., Welland, ON L0B 2R6.
>
> The circumstances of the offence are as follows:

Events Before the Offence

This stage includes any relevant evidence or fact that occurred before the commission of the offence that proves a fact-in-issue or chronologically creates a vivid mental image for the reader.

> On Tuesday, June 6, 2007, the bank opened for business at 09:00 hrs. Four employees worked that day.
>
> At about 15:00 hrs, Lorraine Mattagappo, age 15 yrs, was sitting in the passenger seat of her mother's car that was parked in front of the bank. Her mother entered the bank to make a deposit. Lorraine saw Umbriaggo walking on Main St. He stopped in front of the bank. He put a nylon mask over his head and entered the bank via the front door. He had possession of a .38 calibre Smith and Wesson handgun.
>
> Laura Testadurro, a bank teller, was assigned to wicket #4.

Events During the Offence

This stage describes the *actus reus* that constitutes the offence. The key principles to follow are:

- avoid abstract terms or words—use concrete words and explanations;
- ensure that the content must be relevant to the facts-in-issue;
- structure the events chronologically; and
- use verbatim quotations to describe accused's verbal statements. Do not paraphrase.

> Umbriaggo walked to wicket #4 and pointed the handgun at Mrs. Samson's head and said, "Give me all your money."
>
> Mrs. Testadurro complied by removing $8,000 from the drawer, putting the cash into a canvas bag, and giving the bag to Umbriaggo. The accused person took possession of the canvas bag and ran out the front entrance.

Events After the Offence

This stage includes circumstances that prove the facts-in-issue that occurred after the *actus reus* concluded. The following evidence is applicable to this narrative:

- the possession, disposal, and seizure of physical evidence;
- observations by witnesses relevant to transportation;
- relevant investigative procedures, such as photo line-ups;
- statements made by the accused person to the police or citizens; and
- the date and time of arrest and when the accused was informed of the right to counsel.

Umbriaggo ran toward a parking lot situated at the rear of the bank by using an alley along the west wall of the bank. Bill Skifose, a motorist driving past the bank, saw Umbriaggo enter a parked 2006 white BMW, bearing Ontario Registration WCIB 561.

The police were contacted and an investigation began.

On June 7, 2007, two $10 bills were recovered from a business premises in Welland. The money was identified as having been stolen from the bank. Umbriaggo was identified as having been the possessor of the money.

On June 8, 2007, Lorraine Mattagappo identified Umbriaggo by means of a photo line-up. A section 487 *Criminal Code* search warrant was executed later that day at Umbriaggo's house. A .38 calibre Smith and Wesson handgun, a nylon mask, and a canvas bag were recovered. The canvas bag contained $7,980.

Police arrested Umbriaggo June 8, 2007, for this robbery. He was informed of his right to counsel and was cautioned. He was transported to 51 Division and was interrogated. Umbriaggo gave a written confession to the police.

A bail hearing was conducted. Umbriaggo was released by means of an undertaking with conditions.

Witness Statements

The majority of a Crown Brief is composed of witness statements, written in the format explained in Chapter 9. The witness statements represent the total evidence that will be presented by the prosecution.

One witness statement is necessary for each witness on the witness list. The combined effect of the witness statements must constitute a *prima facie* case. The total evidence must prove that the offender(s) named on the Information committed the offence named on the Information.

PROGRESSING FROM SIMPLE TO COMPLEX CROWN BRIEFS

Learning to write Crown Briefs is accomplished incrementally. Simple Crown Briefs must be mastered before progressing to complex ones. Regardless of the degree of complexity, the same principles and procedures apply as with a simple Crown Brief.

Uniform patrol officers arrest and charge offenders for a wide range of offences. The evidence and circumstances vary significantly. No two offences will be committed in exactly the same way. There always will be some unique evidence or circumstances. Although every Crown Brief has its own distinguishing character and a degree of uniqueness, some will share a number of common facts because of the limited ways in which the offence may be committed. For example, two common offences that uniform patrol officers routinely investigate are:

- theft under $5,000 at department stores (referred in slang terms as "shoplifting"); and
- impaired driving.

These offences will have a number of consistent similar circumstances. Crown Briefs relating to these offences are not complex; they are simple in comparison to other types of Crown Briefs.

The following two sample Crown Briefs (pages 127–137) illustrate how to write summaries and witness statements relating to the common offences.

These samples are followed by a complex Crown Brief (pages 138–148) relating to a bank robbery. Despite the greater complexity of this type of offence, the same principles apply. The summary must establish a *prima facie* case. The witness statements reflect the same procedures and must adhere to the rules of evidence. Essentially, a complex Crown Brief has more witnesses and a greater number of circumstances.

Regina

vs.

Sempro Adruggato

Sample 1   (Continued)

OFFENCE: THEFT UNDER $5,000
                                  SECTION 334(b) *CRIMINAL CODE*

OFFENCE DATE: JULY 1, 2007

ACCUSED PERSON: Sempro ADRUGGATO
                                  1613 Bears St.
                                  WELLAND, Ontario L1E 2F3

                                  (D.O.B. 83–01–10)

OFFENCE LOCATION: CITY OF WELLAND

OFFICER-IN-CHARGE: CST. N. HUDDLE #1100

Sample 1   (Continued)

WITNESSES

1.   Mezzo Matto
      2622 Barton St.
      Welland, Ontario L2E 3F4
      905 836 4382
      or
c/o Niccolo's Department Store
      4424 Machiavelli Ave.
      Welland, Ontario L3E 4F5
      905 369 5407

2.   Cst. N. Huddle #1804
      51 Division
      NRPS

Note to reader: In an actual Crown Brief, the witness list would occupy its own page(s); it would not appear on the same page as the summary.

SUMMARY

This charge arises from an incident that occurred on July 1, 2007, at 2:00 p.m., at Niccolo's Department Store, 4424 Machiavelli Ave., Welland.

The accused person in this matter is Sempro Adruggato, D.O.B. 83–01–10, 1613 Bears St., Welland. He is employed as a bottle loader at Mundo Cardboard Box Inc.

On July 1, 2007, the store opened for business at 10:00 a.m. At 1:50 p.m., Adruggato entered the store and walked through several aisles for ten minutes and selected no items during that time.

At 2:00 p.m., Adruggato entered the electronics department and walked to a CD display. Mezzo Matto, store security, saw Adruggato select a CD with "The Rising" printed on the front.

The CD was valued at $25. Adruggato inserted the CD into his left jacket pocket. He walked to the front entrance, exited the store without paying for the CD, and walked onto the front parking lot.

Matto saw the entire incident and followed Adruggato to the parking lot without losing sight of him. Matto told Adruggato that he was under arrest for Theft under $5,000, informed him of his right to counsel, cautioned him, and told him to accompany Matto inside the store to the security office. Adruggato removed the CD from his jacket pocket, gave it to Matto, and said, "Sorry for stealing it. Can I pay for it now?" Adruggato accompanied Matto to the security office where Matto phoned the police.

Cst. N. Huddle, NRPS, arrived at 2:15 p.m. Cst. Huddle continued the arrest, informed him of the right to counsel and cautioned him. Cst. Huddle asked, "Why did you steal it?" Adruggato answered, "Springsteen is the best musician, 'The Rising' is the best CD, so I stole it."

Cst. Huddle seized the CD. Adruggato was released at 2:35 p.m. by means of an Appearance Notice.

Note to reader: Witness statements follow next. In an actual Crown Brief, each witness statement would occupy its own page(s).

Sample 1   (Continued)

MEZZO MATTO WILL SAY:

I am 25 years old. I live at 2622 Barton Street, Welland, with my parents. I am employed at Niccolo's Department Store, 4424 Machiavelli Ave., Welland, where I hold the position of security guard/retail investigator.

On July 1, 2007, I was working the 10:00 a.m. to 6 p.m. shift, assigned to internal store patrol.

At 1:50 p.m., I saw a male person, who later identified himself to me as Sempro Adruggato, enter the store via the front entrance. I was standing in aisle #6 at the time, 20 metres from the front entrance, and I had a clear view of him. The reason I noticed him was that I recognized him as a past customer. He has been in the store several times in the past but he has never purchased items.

I followed Adruggato for about ten minutes. He walked down four aisles. He looked at several items and put them all back on the shelves. He repeatedly looked from side to side while he was shopping, which heightened my suspicion.

At 2:00 p.m., Adruggato entered the electronics aisle. I stood 20 metres away pretending to shop while I had a clear view of his position. As he stood in front of a CD display, I saw him pick up a CD with "The Rising" printed on the front. He looked to his left and then to his right. He placed the CD into his left jacket pocket. He walked to the front entrance and exited the store without paying for the CD.

I followed him to the parking lot and I stopped him. I had not lost sight of him from the time of the offence until the time of apprehension. I identified myself by name and told him that I was a "store security guard." I said to him, "You're under arrest for theft under $5,000." I read the right to counsel to him from my notebook. I asked him, "Do you understand?"

He replied, "Ya. I don't need a lawyer." I read the caution to him from my notebook and asked, "Do you understand?" He replied, "Ya." I then said to him, "Let's go to the security office inside." Adruggato put his hand in his left jacket pocket, removed the CD, gave it to me and said, "Sorry for stealing it. Can I pay for it now?" I replied, "Come on, let's go," and we walked inside to the security office.

Upon arrival at 2:05 p.m., I phoned the police. I asked for identification. He produced a driver's licence with the name Sempro Adruggato on it. I initialled the plastic cover of the CD. The CD had a $25 sticker on the front. I wrote my note at this time.

At 2:15 p.m., Cst. Huddle arrived at the office. I showed Cst. Huddle my notes and I verbally explained that I saw Adruggato take the CD and leave the store without paying for it. I gave the CD to Cst. Huddle.

I heard Cst. Huddle tell Adruggato, "You're under arrest for theft under $5,000." Cst. Huddle read the right to counsel from a notebook and asked, "Do you understand?" Adruggato replied, "Ya, I already told him I don't want a lawyer." Cst. Huddle read the caution from a notebook and asked, "Do you understand?" Adruggato answered, "Ya, I already told him I understand."

Cst. Huddle asked Adruggato, "Why did you steal it?" Adruggato answered, "Springsteen is the best musician, 'The Rising' is the best CD, so I stole it."

Cst. Huddle asked him questions to complete an arrest report. At 2:35 p.m., Cst. Huddle gave Adruggato an Appearance Notice. Adruggato signed. They both left.

Sample 1   (Concluded)

CST. N. HUDDLE WILL SAY:

I am a member of the Niagara Regional Police Service where I hold the rank of constable. I am assigned to the uniform branch of 51 Division.

On July 1, 2007, I was working the 7 a.m. to 7 p.m. shift, assigned to general patrol duties. As a result of information received from a radio broadcast, I attended at Niccolo's Department Store, 4424 Machiavelli Ave., Welland, at 2:15 p.m. I walked to the security office. Two men were in the office. I identified myself to both men.

Mezzo Matto introduced himself. He gave me a driver's licence with the name Sempro Adruggato on it. Matto gave me a notebook. I read the notes in it. Additionally, he informed me about certain information. Matto gave me a CD with "The Rising" printed on the front. A $25 sticker was on the cover. I saw the initials "MM" on the cover. I seized the CD.

Based on the information I learned, I told Adruggato that he was under arrest for theft under $5,000. I read the right to counsel from my notebook and I asked him, "Do you understand?" Adruggato replied, "Ya, I already told him I don't want a lawyer." I read the caution from my notebook and I asked him, "Do you understand?" He replied, "Ya, I already told him I understand."

I asked Adruggato, "Why did you steal it?" Adruggato replied, "Springsteen is the best musician, 'The Rising' is the best CD, so I stole it."

I asked him questions to complete an arrest report. I completed an Appearance Notice. I explained it to Adruggato and asked him to sign. He signed it and I gave him a copy of it.

I left the store at 2:35 p.m. and arrived at 51 Division at 2:43 p.m. I initialled the cover of the CD and placed it in Locker #4 in the property room.

At 2:51 p.m., I wrote notes relevant to this incident.

Sample 2

Regina

vs.

Jake Umbriaggo

Sample 2 (Continued)

OFFENCE: IMPAIRED DRIVING
                                  SECTION 253 *CRIMINAL CODE*

OFFENCE DATE: JULY 4, 2007

ACCUSED: Jake UMBRIAGGO
                                  6651 Orchard Ave.
                                  WELLAND, Ontario L4E 5F6

                                  (D.O.B. 80–06–06)

OFFENCE LOCATION: CITY OF WELLAND

OFFICER-IN-CHARGE: CST. H. CREIGHTON #362

Sample 2   (Continued)

WITNESSES

1.   Cst. H. Creighton
      #33 Division
      NRP

2.   Cst. E. Sky
      #51 Division
      NRP

SUMMARY

This charge arises from an incident that occurred on July 4, 2007, at 10:15 p.m. on King St. in the city of Welland.

The accused person in this matter is Jake Umbriaggo, D.O.B. 80–06–06, 6651 Orchard Ave., Welland. He is currently employed as a bus driver at Western Air Bus, 5045 Halton Road, Niagara Falls. Umbriaggo owns a 1990 white BMW bearing Ontario registration CLTS 424.

On July 4, 2007, at 10:15 p.m., Umbriaggo was operating his BMW northbound on King St. toward Lincoln St. Cst. Creighton was parked at a gas station on the southwest corner of King St. and Lincoln St. Umbriaggo failed to stop for a red light at Lincoln St. and continued driving northbound on King St.

Cst. Creighton followed the BMW at a distance of 20 metres. The posted speed on King St. is 50 km/h. The BMW was travelling at 70 km/h. The BMW crossed the midline of the roadway and drove onto the southbound lane.

Cst. Creighton activated the roof lights of the cruiser. The BMW returned to the northbound lane and stopped along the east curb of King St. at Division St.

Cst. Creighton walked to the driver's window. Umbriaggo was the only occupant of the car.

Umbriaggo asked Cst. Creighton, "What's the problem?" Cst. Creighton smelled the odour of an alcoholic beverage on Umbriaggo's breath and saw that Umbriaggo's eyes were bloodshot. Umbriaggo's speech was slurred.

Cst. Creighton asked Umbriaggo for his driver's licence, ownership, and insurance. Umbriaggo searched his pockets, removed his wallet, passed his driver's licence three times, and then gave it to the officer. Cst. Creighton told Umbriaggo to exit the car. Umbriaggo opened the door and tripped as he exited.

Cst. Creighton arrested Umbriaggo for Impaired Driving, informed him of the right to counsel, cautioned him, and made a demand for a breath sample.

Umbriaggo was transported to the police station. He provided two breath samples to a qualified technician. Test results showed a BAC of 220 mgs.

The accused person was later released by means of a Promise to Appear.

Sample 2　(Continued)

CST. H. CREIGHTON WILL SAY:

I am a member of the Niagara Regional Police Service, where I hold the rank of constable. I am assigned to the uniform branch of 51 Division.

On July 4, 2007, I was working the 7 p.m. to 7 a.m. shift, assigned to general patrol duties. At 10:15 p.m., I was parked at a gas station situated on the southwest corner of King St. and Lincoln St. I had completed a General Occurrence Report and was preparing to leave that location. As I looked at the traffic on King St., I saw a white BMW travelling north on King St. The car passed First St. and travelled toward Lincoln St. The speed of the car drew my attention to it. The posted speed on King St. is 50 km/h. The car's speed was faster than the other traffic in my view. In my opinion, the BMW was travelling at a speed beyond the posted speed limit.

The traffic light facing northbound traffic on King St. was red. I saw the BMW fail to stop for the red light and travel through the intersection, continuing north on King St. I was parked about 20 metres from the northbound lane. My view was unobstructed. The weather was clear and the roads were dry.

I turned left onto King St. and travelled north following the BMW. When I arrived at a distance of about 10 metres behind the BMW, I saw the plate number—Ontario CLTS 424. The driver was male. He was the lone occupant.

I activated the roof lights of the cruiser. The distance between my cruiser and the BMW remained the same for about two blocks. The cruiser speedometer read 70 km/h.

The BMW crossed the midline of the roadway and travelled partially in the southbound lane for about 50 metres. The car returned to the northbound lane. I saw the brake lights activate. The car stopped near the east curb of King St, about 10 metres south of Division St.

I walked to the driver's window. The window was down. The driver was male, white, about 25 years old, short black hair, black goatee, an earring in his left ear in the shape of a cross, and wearing a purple t-shirt. The driver asked, "What's the problem?" as I leaned toward the driver's door. I smelled the odour of an alcoholic beverage on his breath. His eyes were red. His speech was slurred as he asked the question. I responded by asking him to produce his driver's licence, ownership, and insurance. He searched his front left pant pocket, then his right front pant pocket. He said something that I did not understand. He reached into his left back pant pocket and removed a brown wallet. He opened it and I illuminated it with my flashlight. He searched through the wallet. I saw a driver's licence three times in a plastic folder while he searched. He then removed the driver's licence and gave it to me. The name on the driver's licence was Jake Umbriaggo, D.O.B. 80–06–06, 6651 Orchard Ave., Welland.

I told Umbriaggo to get out of the car. He opened the driver's door. He lifted his left leg to leave the car and fell to the ground. I helped him stand. He was unbalanced as I held his left arm.

I told him he was under arrest for impaired driving. I walked with him to my cruiser and I searched him. Upon completion of the search, he entered the back of my cruiser. I entered the front of the cruiser and read the right to counsel from my notebook. I asked, "Do you understand?" He replied, "Ya, I don't want a lawyer." I read the caution to him from my notebook. I asked him if he understood. Umbriaggo replied, "Ya."

I then read the demand for breath samples to him and asked if he understood. He replied, "What does that mean?" I explained the following: "It means I am demanding that you take a Breathalyzer test and provide two breath samples so that your blood alcohol content can be determined. You have to provide the breath samples. You have no choice. If you refuse, you will be

Sample 2   (Continued)

charged with Refusing to Comply with the Demand. Do you understand?" He replied, "Ya, I'll take the test. I'm not drunk. I only had a couple of beers."

I asked the dispatcher to send a tow truck. At 10:23 p.m., I left the scene of the arrest and drove to the police station. En route, Umbriaggo said, "I only had a couple of beers. I'm not that drunk." His speech was slurred. He then mumbled something that I did not understand. I did not respond. No further conversation occurred.

We arrived at the police station at 10:27 p.m. We entered past the security guard and I led Umbriaggo to the booking room. I asked him questions to complete an arrest report.

At 10:32 p.m., I led Umbriaggo to the Breathalyzer room. I introduced him to Cst. E. Sky and I left the room.

At 10:34 p.m., I wrote notes in my notebook. I completed reports afterward. I returned to patrol at 11:15 p.m.

Sample 2   (Concluded)

CST. E. SKY WILL SAY:

I am a member of the Niagara Regional Police Service, where I hold the rank of constable. I am currently assigned to the Breathalyzer unit. I am a qualified technician. I earned certification on September 15, 1999.

On July 4, 2007, I was working the 7 p.m. to 7 a.m. shift. At 9:37 p.m., I arrived at 51 Division to write statements for a Crown Brief. At 10:23 p.m., I received information and attended at the Breathalyzer room. I prepared the Breathalyzer at that time.

At 10:32 p.m., Cst. H. Creighton arrived at the Breathalyzer room with a male person and introduced him. Cst. Creighton left the room. I asked the accused person for personal information. He identified himself as Jake Umbriaggo.

At 10:40 p.m., Umbriaggo provided a breath sample. The test result showed a BAC of 220 mgs. At 10:57 p.m., Umbriaggo provided a second breath sample. The test result showed a BAC of 220 mgs.

At 11:06 p.m., I lodged Umbriaggo in cell #4. I then completed my notebook and reports.

Sample 3

Regina

vs.

Bill Sparratto

Doug Bastone

Eddie Sporka

Sample 3   (Continued)

OFFENCE:	ROBBERY SECTION 344 *CRIMINAL CODE*
OFFENCE DATE:	JUNE 6, 2007
ACCUSED PERSON:	1. Bill SPARRATTO 1000 King St. THOROLD, Ontario L5F 6G7 (D.O.B. 72–02–05) 2. Doug BASTONE 3000 Lincoln St. THOROLD, Ontario L5G 6H7 (D.O.B. 69–05–25) 3. Eddie SPORKA 800 East Main St. THOROLD, Ontario L5H 6J7 (D.O.B. 69–10–12)
OFFENCE LOCATION:	CITY OF THOROLD
OFFICER-IN-CHARGE:	CST. H. CREIGHTON #362

Sample 3   (Continued)

WITNESSES	SYNOPSIS
1. June Rams 172 Swart Rd. Thorold, Ontario L5J 6K7 or c/o Hill Park High School 66 Valvano St. Thorold, Ontario L5K 6L7	witness outside bank; saw suspects prior to and after robbery
2. George Skifose 836 Brantford Ave. Thorold, Ontario L5L 6M7 or c/o Schmidt Construction 32 Hayes St. Thorold, Ontario L5M 6N7	witnessed plate number of suspect vehicle
3. Wilma Mundo 4424 Essex St. Port Colborne, Ontario L7P 2C3 or c/o National Bank 1804 East Main St. Thorold, Ontario L5N 6P7	bank teller; had gun pointed at her and was robbed of money
4. Gloria Doors 51 Annunziata Ave. Thorold, Ontario L5A 2B4 or c/o National Bank 1804 East Main St. Thorold, Ontario L5N 6P7	bank employee; had knife held to her throat
5. Phylis Bevabeer 23 Artelle Rd. Thorold, Ontario L5B 3C5 or c/o National Bank 1804 East Main St. Thorold, Ontario L5N 6P7	bank teller; had knife pointed at her and was robbed of money
6. Cst. H. Creighton 51 Division NRPS	arresting officer; received confession

Sample 3   (Continued)

SUMMARY

The charges of robbery in this matter arise from an incident that occurred at the National Bank, situated at 1804 East Main St. in the city of Thorold, on June 6, 2007.

The three persons charged with robbery in this matter are

1. Bill Sparratto, D.O.B. 72–02–05, 1000 King St., Thorold

2. Doug Bastone, D.O.B. 69–05–25, 3000 Lincoln St., Thorold

3. Eddie Sporka, D.O.B. 69–10–12, 800 East Main St., Thorold

The circumstances of the offence are as follows:

The bank opened for business at 9:00 a.m. on June 6, 2007. At about 3:00 p.m., Sparratto and Bastone entered the bank via the front entrance while Sporka remained in a van parked behind the bank. The bank was open for business at the time.

Both Sparratto and Bastone wore black nylon stockings over their heads; Sparratto was armed with a knife and Bastone was armed with a handgun. They went to a counter where the bank teller, Wilma Mundo, was working. Mrs. Mundo had been waiting on a customer. Bastone pushed the customer, who was positioned at the counter, and he stood in front of Mrs. Mundo. Bastone held the gun through the wicket, pointed it as Mrs. Mundo, and demanded money.

Sparratto went to the counter near the wicket area where Phylis Bevabeer was working. A bank employee, Gloria Doors, was standing near this area. Sparratto put his arm around Doors's neck and held the knife in front of her face. Sparratto shoved Doors, pointed the knife at her, and instructed her to move away toward a wall. Subsequently, Sparratto pointed the knife to Mrs. Bevabeer and jabbed it toward her as he demanded money.

Both tellers complied and gave Sparratto and Bastone cash from the teller drawers. The money was placed in a bag. The accused persons took possession of the cash and they fled from the bank.

The total amount of money stolen from the bank was $9,000. Included in that amount were twenty $10 bills. Their serial numbers had been previously recorded.

Sparratto and Bastone ran north on an alley adjacent to the bank to a municipal parking lot situated at the back of the bank, on Cross St. They met Sporka who was sitting in the driver's seat of a van bearing Ontario registration BAHA 836, which was parked in the Cross St. parking lot. They entered the van and drove from the scene. The bank alarm was activated. Police officers arrived after the suspects had departed. An investigation commenced.

As a result of the investigation, Sporka was arrested on June 12, 2007. He was cautioned and informed of his right to counsel. During questioning, he verbally admitted to Criminal Investigation Branch officers that he participated in this incident. He gave a written confession implicating Sparratto and Bastone.

Sparratto and Bastone were arrested on June 14, 2007. Both were cautioned and informed of their right to counsel.

During questioning, Sparratto admitted that he participated in this offence and gave a written confession to C.I.B. officers. Bastone verbally admitted that he participated in the offence and explained to C.I.B. officers that he had used a .38 calibre revolver during the commission of the robbery.

Only $20 was recovered.

Bail hearings were later conducted. All three were released by means of undertakings with conditions.

Sample 3   (Continued)

JUNE RAMS WILL SAY:

I am 15 years old. I live at 172 Swart Road, Thorold. I am a grade 9 student at Hill Park High School in Thorold.

On Monday, June 6, 2007, my mother picked me up at school at about 1:30 p.m. in her white BMW. We drove to East Main St., Thorold. We arrived at 2:45 p.m. and parked in front of the National Bank, 1804 East Main St., Thorold. We parked next to the north curb, in front of the restaurant next door to the bank. I was sitting in the front passenger seat. My mother left keys in the ignition and left the ignition on. I stayed inside the car, alone, for about five minutes.

During that time I saw a man standing on the sidewalk in front of the alley next to the bank. He had his hands in his pocket and was looking at me. I can describe him as follows: male, white; 19 years, 5'7", chubby, short dirty blonde hair, clean shaven, bad acne on his face; wearing a one-piece gas station attendant suit, blue in colour. The suit had a little sign on the front but I could not read it. The suit looks the same as the ones worn at a gas station on East Main St., across the street from The Social Club. I can show the gas station to the police. I've been with my mother at that gas station and I'm pretty sure the people there wear the same kind. I would be able to recognize this person if I saw him again.

A second man walked up to #1. The second man came from the alley to meet him. #2 is described as follows: male, white; 6', skinny, short straight brown hair, some facial hair (stubble) and a moustache (thin); heavy knit, crew neck burgundy sweater, black jeans, brown work boots (old).

They both looked directly at me again. I was afraid that they would notice that the car was running. They walked to the front door of the bank and stood outside for a moment. #1, the short man, put black pantyhose over his head. #2, the taller one, also put black pantyhose over his head. I did not see any weapons at this time. I observed their faces for about 15 seconds.

Both went in the bank and I stayed in the car. They were in the bank for about four minutes. They came out of the front entrance of the bank. Both were running. The #2 suspect (tall man) was holding a bank bag. The other man (#1, the short man) was holding a knife and a gun. The knife had a blade about 12" long and a brown handle; it looked like a jackknife. The gun was brown and looked fake. The barrel was very short. Both men ran to the alley, and ran north, down the alley, along the side of the bank.

At 3:05 p.m., a police detective arrived with several officers. He interviewed me briefly and I informed him about what I saw. At 4:00 p.m., I was interviewed at the police station and gave the detective a written statement.

On Tuesday, June 7, 2007, at 9:00 a.m., I attended at the police station and was met by the detective. He showed me a photo line-up composed of 12 photographs. He instructed me to "Look at each photograph and point to one who you recognize." I looked at each photograph. I pointed to #4. I recognized the man in that photograph as suspect #2 who I saw in front of the bank.

Sample 3   (Continued)

WILMA MUNDO WILL SAY:

My name is Wilma Mundo. I am 31 years old and live at 4424 Essex St., Port Colborne with my husband and two children.

I work as a part-time teller at National Bank at 1804 East Main St., Thorold. I have worked here for two years.

On June 6, 2007, I was working at the National Bank from 9 a.m. to 5 p.m. At approximately 3:00 p.m., I was at my wicket and I was waiting on a customer.

I then heard yelling. I looked up. The customer was being pushed out of the way by a man.

The man was wearing a black nylon mask over his head. He was approximately 6' tall, 170 lbs., and may have had light brown hair. He was wearing something blue and may have been in his early 20s. I saw a second man who also entered the bank and was wearing a black nylon stocking over his head. The second man did not come to my wicket. He was shorter (approx. 5'6") and looked to be in his 30s.

The first man, who pushed my customer out of the way, came up to my counter and pointed a gun at me in between the wicket. He then said, "Give me the money now!" He kept jabbing the gun toward me, moving it up and down.

I started to take all the money out of my top drawer. It contained $10 and $20 bills. The man then yelled, "No not that, the bottom drawer, the large stuff!!" I gave him the money in the bottom drawer. While I did that, he kept saying, "Give me more, I want it all." The money that I gave him included "bait" money that the bank keeps record of the serial numbers for so the money is traceable. The "bait" money I gave him consisted of ten $10 bills.

He kept yelling for more money so I began to gather my $5 bills, but he ran out of the bank without taking them. The other man who had been at another wicket also ran out of the bank at the same time he did. The one that was at my wicket took approximately $4,000 in total.

I cannot facially recognize either suspect.

Sample 3   (Continued)

GLORIA DOORS WILL SAY:

My name is Gloria Doors. I am 46 years old and I live at 51 Annunziata Ave., Thorold with my husband. I am the assistant manager of Commercial Credit at the National Bank at 1804 East Main St., Thorold. I have been employed there for seven years.

On Monday, June 6, 2007, I was working at the National Bank located at 1804 East Main St., Thorold. At approximately 3:00 p.m. I was in the main lobby of the bank, standing by Barb Smith's wicket, talking to a customer.

All of a sudden, someone put their arm around my neck and held a knife in front of my face with their left hand. The person who was holding me then turned me toward the front door, and I saw another man run into the bank. He was wearing a black nylon stocking over his head and was holding a handgun that seemed to have a long barrel.

The man who was holding me then shoved me away from him and pointed the knife at me and said, "Get back against the wall, move it!" He jabbed the knife toward me and then pointed it toward the teller, Phylis Bevabeer.

I stayed against the wall and just watched him. He demanded money from Phylis and she gathered it for him. He was 25 to 30 years old. He was around 5'10" or 5'11" tall and weighed approximately 150 lbs. He had on a black nylon stocking over his head. It looked like he had sandy blond or light brown hair. His lips were skinny and his teeth were rotten on the left hand side, on the top. He was wearing light blue jeans that were faded from washing. He had on black vinyl runners with a name on the side that I could not see. He had on a brown/olive coloured shaker knit sweater.

The knife was a hunting knife, about 10" long. It has a wide silver blade that was slightly curved at the end.

After Phylis gave him all the money, he picked it up and then ran out with the other man, who had also entered the bank in a black nylon stocking mask.

I then ran to the door to see which way they were going, but they were already out of sight. A customer that was outside the door, just coming into the bank, said that they had run down the alley.

I cannot facially recognize the suspects.

Sample 3   (Continued)

PHYLIS BEVABEER WILL SAY:

I am 29 years old and I live at 23 Artelle Rd., Thorold, with my husband and my daughter. I work at the National Bank, 1804 East Main Street, Thorold. I have been employed there for nine years.

On Monday, June 6, 2007, I was working from 9 a.m. to 5 p.m. At approximately 3:05 p.m. or 3:10 p.m., I was looking down into my cash drawer when I heard a commotion right in front of my wicket. As I looked up, I saw a guy with a black ladies' stocking over his head. At first I didn't take it seriously, but he was jabbing a knife at me. The knife looked like a hunting knife—about 6–7" long and 1" wide. While jabbing the knife, he demanded my large bills. He repeatedly said, "Large bills, large bills, give me your large bills."

He looked like he had dirty blond hair, which was straight and hanging out of the stocking at the back. He was about 5'10" or 5'11" tall with a thin build. He was wearing a dark greenish/mustard coloured tweed sweater with a round neck. I believed by his voice that he was about 25 years old. He had no accent.

I gathered the large bills from my bottom drawer and gave him four $100 bills and two $50 bills. He wasn't satisfied with that, and he then shouted, "I want all of it." I then gave him $1,000 in $20 bills and $2,500 in $5 bills. He shouted, "I want more large, more large." And I told him I didn't have any. Then he said, "I want more money." So I gave him my $20 bills, $10 bills, and my "bait" money that the bank keeps the serial numbers for. The "bait" money consisted of ten $10 bills. He then turned and ran out of the bank.

Periodically, while gathering my money, I was looking at Wilma Mundo, who was two wickets to my left. The guy in front of her was pointing a gun at her. I think it was a revolver with a long barrel.

I had approximately $2,750 stolen from my drawers.

I did not see the man who had the gun very well and I don't remember what he looked like. I cannot facially recognize the suspects.

Sample 3   (Continued)

GEORGE SKIFOSE WILL SAY:

I am 21 years old. I live at 836 Brantford Ave., Thorold. I am employed as a labourer at Jerry's Construction, 32 Hayes St., Thorold.

On Monday, June 6, 2007, I worked from 7 a.m. to 3 p.m. at Jerry's Construction. At about 2:55 p.m., I left work on my motorcycle. I was on my way home. East Main St. is always on my route home from work.

At about 3:00 p.m., I was travelling westbound on East Main St. As I drove toward the National Bank, I saw one man running into the alley next to the bank. At that time I was in the right lane, travelling about 50 km/h. When I saw the man, I was about 20 metres away from the bank's front entrance, approaching it from the east side. I had a clear, unobstructed view of this man. He was holding a bag. He was wearing a black stocking over his head. The guy ran north down the alley. I can't remember anything else he was wearing.

I turned right onto the last street near the canal, toward the municipal parking lot on Cross St., behind the bank. I turned right onto the Cross St. parking lot. I saw a white van that was stopped behind X Fitness. I was about 20 metres from the van. I had a clear view of the back of the van only. The van started moving, and travelled east toward Cross St. I followed it. I didn't see any other vehicles moving. There were no cars between us. The van turned right onto Cross St. and travelled south to East Main St. It stopped for a red light. I stopped directly behind it. I had a clear, unobstructed view of the back plate. The plate number was BAHA 836. I believe it was a Chevy van, late 90s, no side window. I drove toward the right curb and stopped on the right side of the van, next to the front passenger door. I took a very fast look and I'm pretty sure I saw only the driver, who looked like a young male. The light was red for about thirty seconds. When the light turned green, the van crossed East Main St., travelling south. I turned right onto East Main St. and drove home. My house is situated only two blocks from that intersection.

I arrived home and entered the house via the front door. I walked into the kitchen and wrote the plate number BAHA 836 onto a white piece of paper that was on the table. It took me about four minutes to get home and write the plate number after I read the plate.

At 7:50 p.m. I went to the Thorold Police Station and I gave the piece of paper to Cst. H. Creighton. I was interviewed and gave a written statement.

Sample 3　(Continued)

CST. H. CREIGHTON WILL SAY:

I am a member of the Niagara Regional Police Service where I hold the rank of detective constable. I am assigned to the Criminal Investigation Branch of 51 Division.

On Monday, June 6, 2007, I was working the 7:00 a.m. to 7:00 p.m. shift. As a result of information received, I attended at the National Bank, 1804 East Main St., Thorold, at 3:14 p.m. Upon arrival, I was met by June Rams. She was standing on the sidewalk outside the bank. She informed me of certain information.

I entered the bank and received information from three uniform officers. At 3:38 p.m., I departed from the bank and arrived at 51 Division, where I interviewed June Rams. She dictated a statement and I wrote it.

At 7:50 p.m., I was at 51 Division. George Skifose attended there. I interviewed him. He dictated a statement and I wrote it. At 8:03 p.m., he gave me a white piece of paper with "BAHA 836" written on it. I placed this in an envelope. I initialled the envelope and placed it in property locker #18.

At 8:00 a.m., June 7, 2007, I prepared a photo line-up. At 9:00 a.m., June Rams attended at 51 Division. I interviewed her briefly in interview room #2. I presented her with the photo line-up. I instructed her to "Look at all 12 photos. Point to anyone who you recognize." After about one minute, she pointed to photo #4 and informed me of certain information.

At 10:00 a.m., I attended at 3000 Lincoln St. I knocked on the front door. A man answered. I identified myself verbally and presented my badge. The following conversation occurred:

HC: Can I come in?

DB: Sure.

HC: Are you Doug Bastone?

DB: Yes.

HC: You are under arrest for a robbery that occurred yesterday at the National Bank on East Main St.

DB: Listen, it wasn't my idea.

HC: (read the right to counsel from a card) Do you understand?

DB: Ya, I don't want a lawyer.

HC: Do you wish to say anything in answer to the charge? You are not obliged to say anything unless you wish to do so, but whatever you say may be used in evidence. Do you understand?

DB: Ya.

HC: We're going to the police station. (I searched him and led him to my cruiser, where he sat in the back.)

At 10:06 a.m., I drove from the house to the police station. En route, the following conversation occurred:

DB: I've never done anything like this. It wasn't my idea.

HC: Where's the money?

DB: It's gone. Bill paid a guy. He owed money.

We arrived at 51 Division at 10:11 a.m. I led him to interview room #4. The following conversation occurred:

HC: Why did you rob the bank?

DB: Bill pressured me. I wasn't thinking.

HC: Do you want to give me a written statement about what happened?

DB: Ya, I'll tell you the whole story.

Sample 3   (Concluded)

At 10:16 a.m., he dictated a statement. I wrote it. It concluded at 10:33 a.m. I gave it to him to read. He signed it. I placed him in cell #32.

At 11:00 a.m., I attended at 1000 King St. Bill Sparratto was on the sidewalk in front of the house. I identified myself. I told him he was under arrest for the robbery at the National Bank. I led him to my cruiser, searched him, and he sat in the back. I read the right to counsel from a card and asked if he understood. He answered, "Yes." I read the caution and asked if he understood. He replied, "Ya." We departed at 11:05 a.m. and arrived at 51 Division at 11:09 a.m. No conversation occurred during that time. I led him to interview room #13. The following conversation occurred:

HC: Whose idea was it to rob the bank?
(No response)
HC: Did you owe someone money? Is that the reason why you robbed the bank?
BS: I panicked. I had to get the money.
HC: Do you want to give me a written statement?
BS: I already told you.

At 11:12 a.m., the statement commenced. It ended at 11:17 a.m. He signed it. I lodged him in cell #13.

At 12:00 p.m., I attended at the front desk of 51 Division as a result of information received. A man was there. I identified myself. I asked him for his name. He answered, "Eddie Sporka." I arrested him for robbery at the National Bank. I read the right to counsel to him and asked if he understood. He answered, "Yes. I don't want a lawyer." I read the caution to him and asked if he understood. He answered, "Ya, I want to tell my side of the story." I led him to interview room #18. I asked him if he wanted to give a written statement, He said, "Sure." The statement commenced at 12:08 p.m. and it concluded at 12:16 p.m. I lodged him in cell #18.

Glossary

10-code language   A numeric language where numbers beginning with "10" replace a specific term, such as "10-8" (in service). *(Ch. 6)*

Abstract language   Words or phrases that have multiple interpretations. *(Ch. 5)*

Actus reus   The physical act of an offence. *(Ch. 6)*

Arrest report   Similar to a GOR, with only one difference: an arrest, by definition, was made during the investigation. *(Ch. 1)*

Briefing   A platoon meeting conducted prior to the beginning of a tour of duty. *(Ch. 6)*

Circumstantial evidence   A series of events or situations that lead to a logical conclusion or opinion, in the absence of direct evidence such as eyewitness observation. *(Ch. 6)*

Concrete language   Words or phrases that have a single interpretation. *(Ch. 5)*

Crown Brief   A formal written record of existing evidence that supports a charge against an accused person. *(Ch. 1)*

Disclosure   The divulging of all relevant material by the Crown to the accused/defence. *(Ch. 10)*

EBA cycle   A cycle of analyzing *evidence*, forming a corresponding *belief*, and taking corresponding *action*. *(Ch. 1)*

Ebbinghaus's Forgetting Curve   The result of a memory retention study conducted by Hermann Ebbinghaus, which concluded that while memory decays steeply rather than gradually, conscious review dramatically slows the rate of forgetting. *(Ch. 6)*

Exculpatory statement   An alibi or denial by a suspect. *(Ch. 6)*

***Ex parte* hearing**   A hearing that takes place during the laying of an Information, in which an officer or complainant meets with a justice of the peace, in the absence of the accused, with the objective of proving by reasonable grounds that the accused committed an offence. *(Ch. 6)*

Eyewitness observation   An observation made when the *actus reus*—the physical act that occurred during the offence—is seen. *(Ch. 6)*

Facts-in-issue (FII)   The elements that compose an offence. *(Ch. 2)*

General Occurrence Report (GOR)   The initial report of a criminal offence, provincial offence, or any other incident that requires a police investigation, such as sudden deaths and missing persons. *(Ch. 1)*

GOS model   A report-writing model composed of *goals*, *objectives*, and *strategies*. *(Ch. 2)*

Hearsay evidence   Content reported by a witness as recorded by a police officer. *(Ch. 6)*

IBDA   A process for writing the narrative sequence of *introduction*, *before the occurrence*, *during the occurrence*, and *after the occurrence*. *(Ch. 2)*

Inculpatory statement   An incriminating statement made by a suspect. *(Ch. 6)*

Independent witness   A witness to an event, other than the complainant. *(Ch. 6)*

Indictable offence   An offence classified as a major criminal offence. *(Ch. 7)*

In service   The formal term referring to "on patrol" or "on the air available for calls." *(Ch. 6)*

Laying an Information   The completion of a document used to charge an adult or young offender, the contents of which are sworn under oath; if reasonable grounds prove the offence committed by the person named, a formal charge is made once the Information is signed by a justice. *(Ch. 7)*

Long-term recall   A secondary, permanent memory system; permits information storage for a lifetime. *(Ch. 6)*

Mens rea   The mental element of an offence; the intent to commit an offence. *(Ch. 6)*

Narrative   The part of any type of police literature that actively explains the specific, relevant circumstances. *(Ch. 1)*

Notebook   The first literature written in most investigations. *(Ch. 1)*

Offence/occurrence recognition (OR)   A skill that involves analyzing a set of circumstances, determining whether or not an offence has occurred, and identifying the offence if so. *(Ch. 2)*

Out of service   The formal term referring to "unavailable to respond to calls for service." *(Ch. 6)*

Prima facie case   A case in which all the facts-in-issue have been proven beyond a reasonable doubt. *(Ch. 3)*

Reasonable doubt   The legal standard of belief that results in an acquittal. *(Ch. 10)*

Relevance   Any information that has some use to the defence. *(Ch. 5)*

RSP system   A communication strategy that systematically governs the writing of narratives through *relevance, structure,* and *precision. (Ch. 2)*

Short-term recall   A primary, temporary memory system for new information. *(Ch. 6)*

Summary   A narrative that explains the commission of an offence and establishes a *prima facie* case. *(Ch. 3)*

Summary conviction offence   An offence classified as a minor criminal offence. *(Ch. 7)*

Verbatim   Word-for-word; a direct quote. *(Ch. 5)*

Witness statement   Formal written records of witness observations that are relevant to the offence or incident. *(Ch. 1)*

Index